North Carolina Governor RICHARD CASWELL

Founding Father and Revolutionary Hero

JOE A. MOBLEY

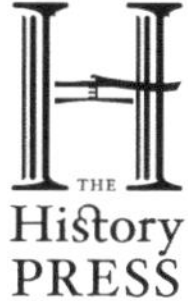

Published by The History Press
Charleston, SC
www.historypress.net

First published 2016

Manufactured in the United States

ISBN 978.1.46713.544.3

Library of Congress Control Number: 2016938315

To the memory of my brother Steve

Contents

Acknowledgements

I wish to acknowledge a number of persons who provided assistance in the production of this book. To historian William C. Harris, my teacher and mentor, I express my gratitude for reading a version of the manuscript and, as always, offering sound advice. I am also indebted to the staff of the Southern Historical Collection of Wilson Library at the University of North Carolina at Chapel Hill and to the staff of the State Archives of North Carolina at Raleigh, especially Kim Andersen, head of the Audio Visual Materials Unit. All illustrations in the book are from that agency. Recognition has to go to the late W. Keats Sparrow, a committed and generous supporter of North Carolina history, for his volume *"The First of Patriots and Best of Men": Richard Caswell in Public Life* (2007), which is an annotated version of the PhD dissertation "The Public Life of Richard Caswell," written by Clayton Brown Alexander in 1930. I hope that my book helps to fulfill Dr. Sparrow's call for further investigation of the career of Richard Caswell. Most of all, I thank my wife, Kathleen B. Wyche (Kay), for proofreading and correcting the draft. Her advice, encouragement and editorial skill are always essential and much appreciated.

Introduction

When one reflects on the Founding Fathers of the United States, North Carolina does not immediately come to mind. It is true that as North Carolina moved toward independence, statehood and a role in establishing the new nation, it did not produce a national political leader of the reputation of a Washington, Adams, Franklin, Hamilton, Jefferson or Madison. In this regard, North Carolina was overshadowed by other colonies, such as Virginia and Massachusetts. Perhaps more than any other factor, the colony's slowly developing economy was the reason for that situation.

A number of elements contributed to a weak economy in "poor Carolina": the lack of a large and profitable staple crop, a primitive transportation system, a shortage of labor and hard currency and, perhaps most of all, a coastal geography—marked by the barrier sand islands known as the Outer Banks—that produced shallow sounds and dangerous inlets and capes and denied the colony deepwater harbors, essential for a thriving maritime commerce. "By the close of the colonial period," writes historian A. Roger Ekirch, "North Carolina's economy was more expansive and prosperous than it had been in earlier years. . . . Yet the economy was still underdeveloped during the last decades of British rule. Progress had been achieved during the eighteenth century, but economic prospects remained checkered."[1]

Directly tied to the sluggish growth of the colony's economy was the slow rise of an elite class of strong political leaders. As historian William S. Price Jr. has summarized, "A small-scale economy, a dearth of educational institutions, and a social and political leadership bent on making money

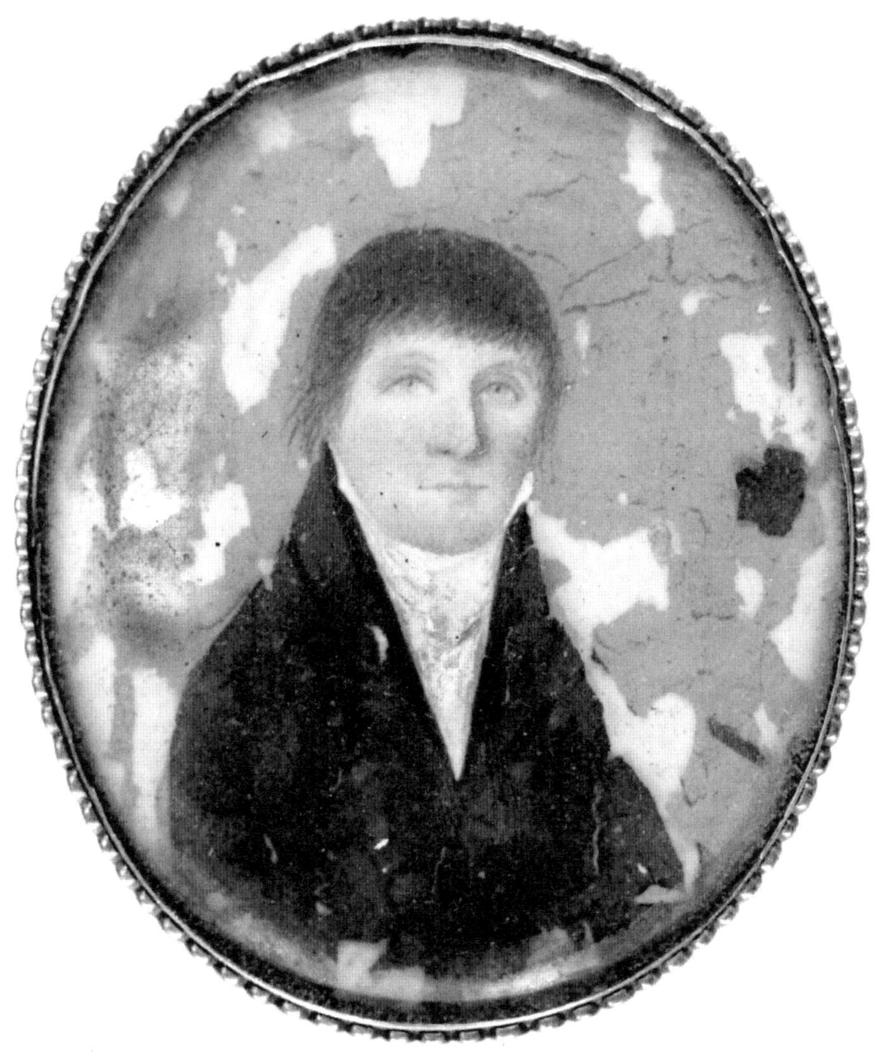

This image was once thought to show Richard Caswell. Now it is generally believed that he is not the subject.

fast meant that North Carolina on the eve of the Revolution would have no figures like Washington, Jefferson, and Madison; nor did it have a cosmopolitan city like Charleston, with its sophisticated cultural life."[2]

Nevertheless, despite its early handicaps, North Carolina produced a number of vital political and military leaders in the struggle for American independence and the founding of the new nation. One such figure was Richard Caswell, the first governor of the *state* of North Carolina. A close examination of Caswell's career broadens our understanding of the American Revolution and the building of a nation in its aftermath. During the war, the Continental Congress and the Continental army of General George Washington relied heavily on state governments and their militias for financial and military support to carry the fight to the enemy and keep the struggle for liberty alive. Once independence was secured through battlefield victory, the adoption of the United States Constitution and the freedoms it bestowed and protected depended on ratification by the individual states. In both efforts, North Carolina's Richard Caswell played a decisive role.

His accomplishments as governor, legislator and military commander exemplify the contributions made to the national cause by North Carolina's political and military leaders during the Revolutionary era. As did other founders of the Republic, he began his career as a loyal British subject and colonial official, with a strong allegiance to the monarchy and its laws. But as Caswell came to believe that the rights of Americans as British subjects were being threatened by Parliament's new colonial policies, he broke his ties to the Crown, embraced a revolutionary fervor, answered the call for American independence and helped forge a new democratic nation. How his life and those events unfolded is the subject of the chapters that follow.

Chapter 1

A Loyal Subject of the British Crown

Richard Caswell was born on August 3, 1729, at the seaport of Joppa, the county seat of Baltimore County, Maryland. He grew up with his parents, Richard Caswell Sr. and Christian Dallam Caswell, and several brothers and sisters at the family plantation, Mulberry Point, located north of the town. His father—descended from English gentry—had migrated from London to Maryland, arriving on February 2, 1712. There he became a successful planter and merchant, county court justice, coroner, militia captain, legislator and vestryman at St. John's (Anglican) Church. At Joppa, Richard Caswell Jr. attended the parish school of the Reverend William Cawthorn and the Reverend Joseph Hooper of St. John's Church.

When his father's health failed around 1743, Richard and his brother William (the eldest sons) took over the management of the family's plantation and mercantile business. But when Joppa declined as a seaport, so did the Caswells' own finances, and the elder Richard Caswell sold his real estate to his brother-in-law, William Dallam, in 1745. The family then intended to follow relatives to North Carolina to seek recovery of their fortunes. But because of Richard Sr.'s ill health, most of the family remained in Maryland. Only Richard Jr. and William traveled to North Carolina to find work, acquire land and establish a place for the rest of the family to join them.

Bearing a letter of recommendation from the governor of Maryland to the governor of North Carolina, Richard and William arrived at New Bern in late 1745. The elder Richard Caswell and the rest of his family soon followed to New Bern, where the father began operating an ordinary. William

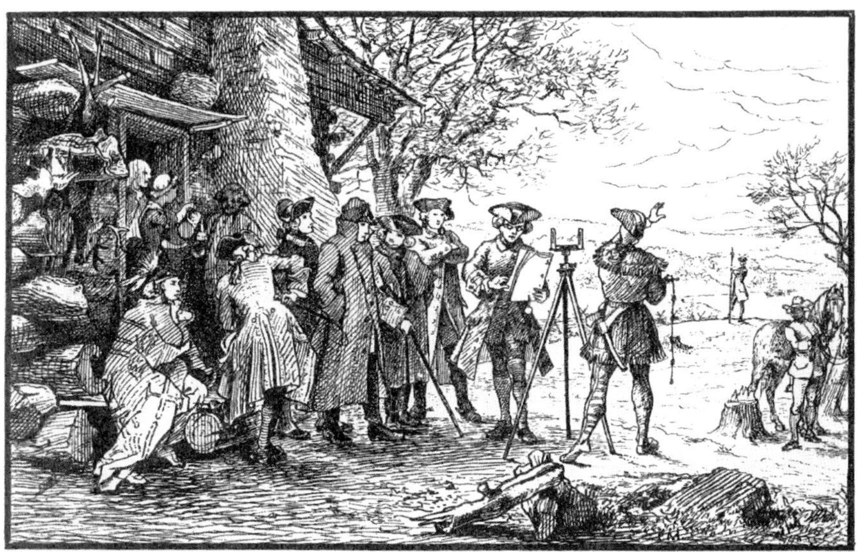

Caswell began his career as a land surveyor.

obtained employment as deputy clerk of the Johnston County Court after that county was formed from Craven County in 1746. At age seventeen, the ambitious Richard Jr. became an apprentice to James Mackilwean, North Carolina's surveyor general. He lived with the Mackilweans for two years at their plantation, Tower Hill, on the Neuse River. Then he became deputy surveyor general, and he acquired a small plantation and built a residence at what is now the town of Kinston. Caswell originally named his new home The Hill but changed it to Newington-on-the-Hill some years later. (It became known as Vernon Hall in 1840.) His extended family moved there in 1748, and brother William resigned his position as deputy clerk to manage the plantation. Caswell's father, Richard Sr., took over William's place as deputy clerk, rising to become clerk and eventually a justice of Johnston County before he died in 1755 and was buried at Newington-on-the-Hill.

By 1747, the young Richard Caswell had been introduced to politics and political leaders in colonial North Carolina by James Mackilwean, who was a member of the Colonial Assembly, as well as surveyor general, and his neighbor Dr. Francis Stringer, a local business owner and also a member of the assembly.[1] Caswell soon became an officer in the Johnston County militia and served as deputy clerk of the county from

1749 to 1753. For a few weeks in the latter year, he held the office of clerk of court for the new county of Orange—which had been formed the previous year from parts of Johnston, Bladen and Granville Counties—before resigning to become high sheriff of Johnston County.[2] According to one authority on Caswell, C.B. Alexander, it was while serving as county clerk, "recording the many details of court proceedings and copying and issuing all kinds of legal papers and writs, that he became familiar with the workings of the machinery of the law and acquired that exact knowledge of the merits and defects of the system." As sheriff, "he seems to have fulfilled the duties of this office with more than the usual diligence, for he was allowed an extra reward of eight pounds for having rendered a full account of taxes, the collection of which made up such an important part of the sheriff's duties."[3]

In 1754, the voters of Johnston County elected Caswell to the Colonial Assembly, a position he held until the American Revolution, presiding as Speaker of the house of commons in 1770–71. While launching his political career in North Carolina, the young Caswell married Mary Mackilwean, the daughter of James and Elinor Mackilwean, on April 21, 1752. The couple had three children. One daughter died at birth in 1753. A son, William, born in 1754, lived to gain some fame as a general of militia during the American Revolution. Another daughter, born in 1757, died in infancy, and Mary Mackilwean died that same year from complications of childbirth. During their brief marriage, the Caswells lived at Red House plantation, recently acquired by Caswell and also in present-day western Kinston. She was buried there. (Throughout their lifetimes, Caswell and his family resided at various sites on his Dobbs County lands.)

Around the same time, Caswell started reading law under the tutelage of William Herritage, a leading attorney in colonial North Carolina and clerk of the Colonial Assembly from 1738 to 1769. On June 20, 1758, Caswell married his second wife, Sarah Herritage, daughter of his mentor, William Herritage. The couple established a residence at Woodington, a plantation near present-day Kinston. Their marriage produced eight children, seven of whom survived to adulthood. Caswell was admitted to the bar in 1759 and began a four-year term as deputy attorney general while also serving in the assembly.[4]

As a member of the Colonial Assembly, he proposed and supported much important legislation. To bolster trade and commerce and overcome the primitive conditions that inhibited economic growth, he introduced a number of bills. In his first year, he proposed an act that established ferries at several locations and mandated that district commissioners build roads to the ferries. He introduced a bill in 1758 that called for improvements in road-building methods. To the bill creating Dobbs County from Johnston County he added a provision for the construction of more roads and ferries. To promote commerce and improve navigation on the Neuse River, he backed an act requiring local justices to construct four warehouses near the river. He secured an exemption from paying duty on gunpowder and lead for shipowners and shipbuilders in North Carolina, a measure intended to aid shipping interests. In an effort to improve the declining tobacco trade, Caswell pushed through the assembly a law to eliminate the export of inferior tobacco by requiring planters to have their tobacco inspected at warehouses at Atkins Bank in Dobbs County before shipment. In 1762, he introduced the bill that established the town of Kingston at Atkins Bank. The name honored King George III but was changed to Kinston after the American Revolution. Caswell served as one of the commissioners who planned the town and, because of his experience as a surveyor, might have helped lay out the street grid. Soon afterward, he built a house in Kingston, which he painted red like his Red Hill dwelling.

Other legislation authored by Caswell included a bill in 1757 that reestablished an old law against gambling. It limited the amount a gambler could win in twenty-four hours to five shillings, except when betting on horse races, a popular pastime of the gentry in which he probably participated because he had a fondness for fine horses. The law also prohibited tavern keepers from allowing games except backgammon, under the threat of loss of license and a fine. Caswell introduced a bill in 1768 for encouraging iron

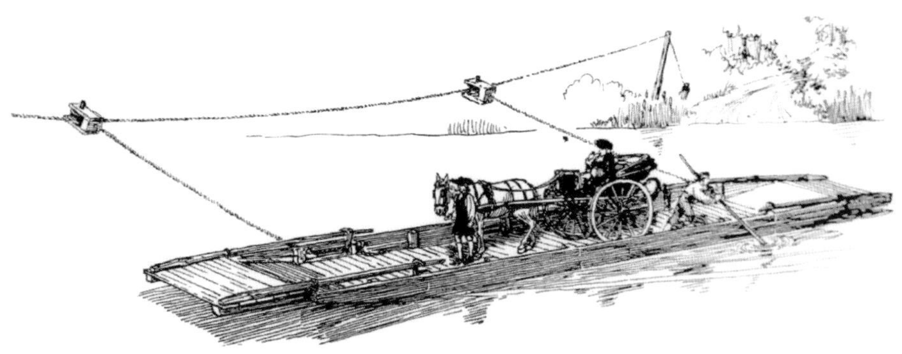

As a member of the Colonial Assembly, Caswell supported the building of ferries.

manufacturing in Chatham County, but the industry did not achieve much until the wartime demands of the Revolution. He also favored the production of raw silk in North Carolina, but such an enterprise never developed.[5]

Caswell played a significant role in the financial affairs of the colonial government of North Carolina. Shortly after taking his seat in the assembly, he served on a committee to write legislation to reform the system of land survey and sales, including improvements in recordkeeping and collection of quitrents. During the French and Indian War (1754–63), he served on a committee to raise £4,000 to defend the frontier of the colony from Indian attack. Wary of the government's previous practice of issuing paper money that tended to depreciate in value, he suggested that the sum be raised from interest-bearing treasury notes to be guaranteed by a poll and other taxes. The redeemable notes proved a success, and the method was followed in a number of future government enterprises, thereby avoiding the perils of issuing paper money for those projects. He endorsed or proposed other legislation to raise money to supply recruits, equipment, weapons and gunpowder in the British fight against the French in the Ohio River Valley and against Indian attack in western North Carolina. In 1756, he, along with two other legislators, visited and inspected Fort Dobbs near present-day Statesville and made recommendations for its improvement and supplies. The fort was built in that year to defend against Indian attack on the western frontier and manned by provincial rangers under Hugh Waddell. It was attacked only once, by the Cherokee in February 1760. Around twelve Indian warriors were killed, and the white defenders lost one or two men.

In 1758, Caswell introduced legislation regarding distribution of funds allocated by Parliament for reimbursing the southern colonies for the expenses they incurred during the war. But trouble erupted between the assembly and Governor Arthur Dobbs, who wanted to draw on the money without consulting the house of commons about its allocation. That resulted in a reduced amount of money given to North Carolina compared to other colonies and led to bad feelings between the house and the governor. Further requests for money by Dobbs were denied by Caswell and his committee.

Conflict over the use of government funds continued when Caswell headed a committee for the auditing of the public accounts. Audits led the assembly to command the treasurer not to pay out any money to the governor or his council without the approval of the North Carolina House of Commons. Further, in 1761, the colonial lawmakers censured Dobbs to the British Privy Council for not explaining to the house the reasons for which he had withdrawn funds from the treasury. In 1773, the assembly

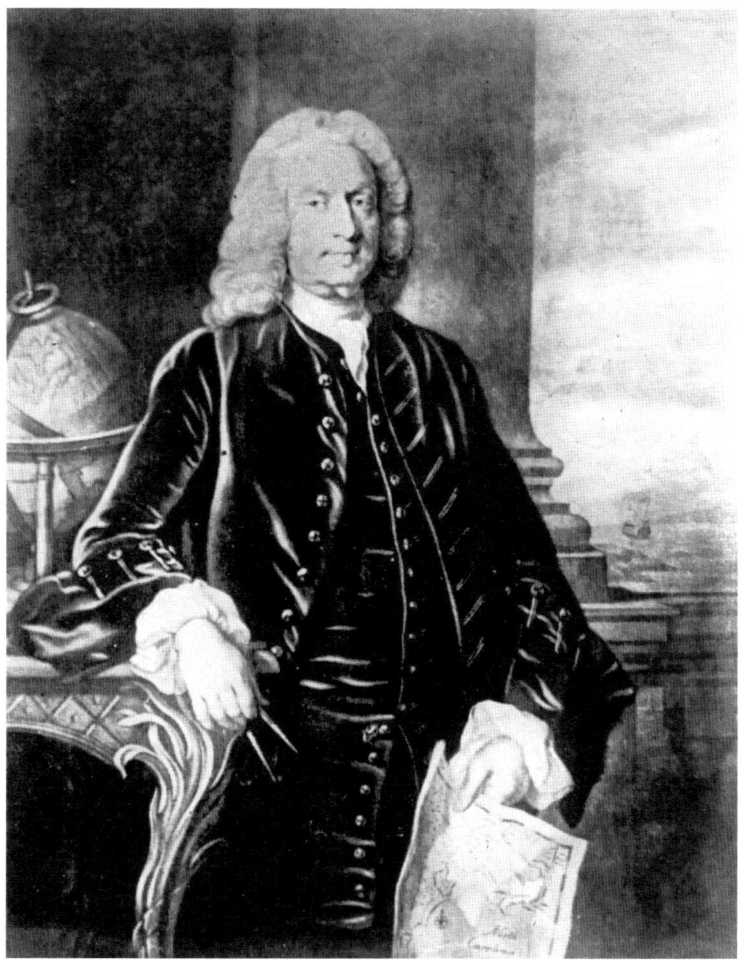

Governor Arthur Dobbs.

appointed Caswell treasurer of the Southern District of North Carolina, with responsibility to collect taxes from the sheriffs of a number of counties, a task he performed with diligence.[6]

As a member of the assembly, Caswell supported or advocated several humanitarian or public welfare measures. In 1762, he proposed an amendment to a 1749 law concerning the release of insolvent debtors who were in prison. His amendment provided for a speedier release of the debtors, and it lowered the colony's cost of keeping them imprisoned. He also was instrumental in securing the passage of a new law specifying a special court session to deal with orphans and mandating that a grand jury assume the responsibility for orphans previously cared for by church wardens.[7] As a committee member in late 1773, he approved of maintaining the Anglican vestry act for poor relief, with an amendment stipulating that if the vestry should neglect the poor, the county court would have the authorization to

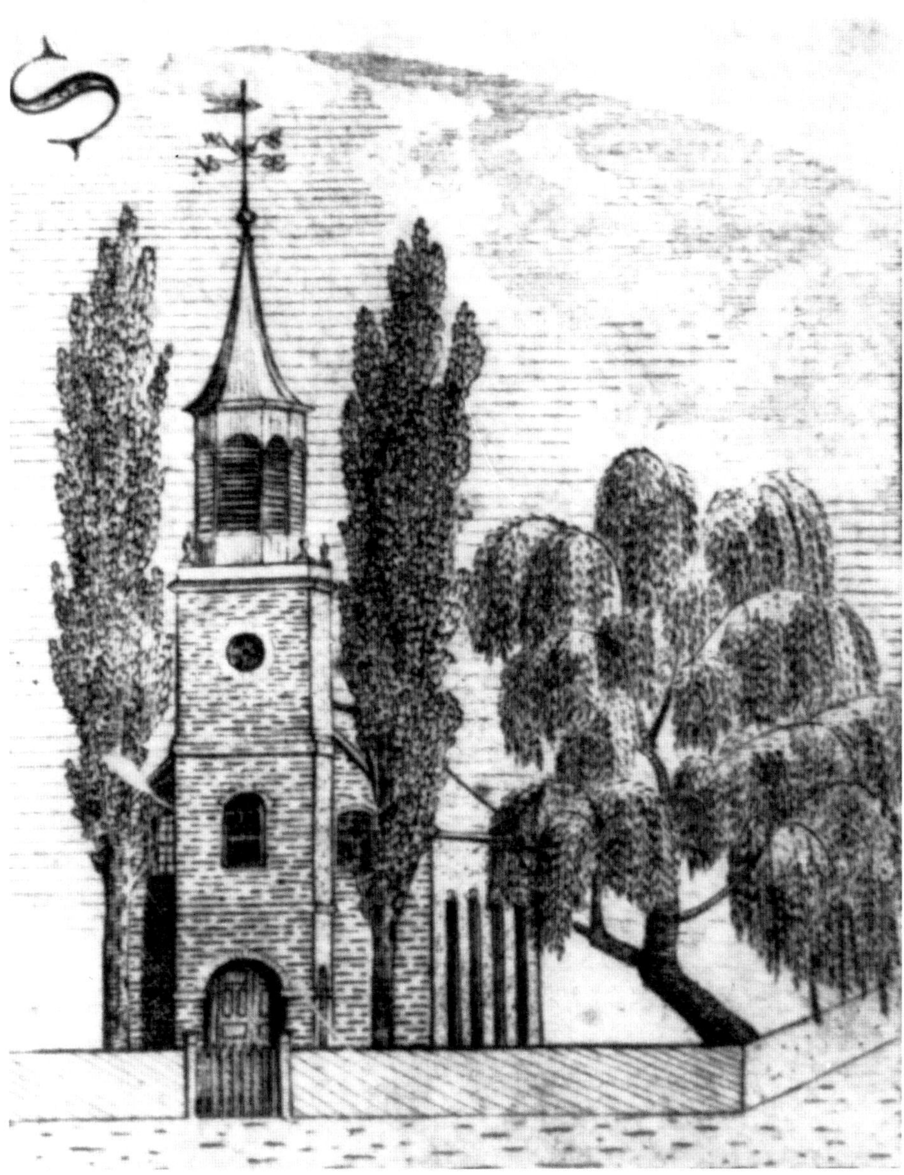

Caswell attended the old Christ Church in New Bern. At his death, a memorial service was held there.

provide aid because the destitute "ought always to be one of the principal objects of legislation." Caswell was himself Anglican (Episcopalian after the American Revolution) and, at various times, attended both St. Matthew's Church in Kingston and Christ Church in New Bern.[8]

Particularly noteworthy for his time and place was Caswell's support for public education in North Carolina. As a legislator, he proposed "erecting and establishing a free-school for every county," initially using funds awarded to the colony by the Crown for services provided during the French and Indian War. According to one authority, Charles L. Holloman, his "'Address of the General Assembly,' sent to the king in 1760, was cited to legislatures for many decades thereafter on behalf of free public schools."[9]

One of Caswell's greatest contributions while serving in the Colonial Assembly was court reform. He became the chief spokesman for the Court Bill of 1762, an act that the assembly would renew every two years. The bill called for improvements in the operations of the clerks of inferior and superior courts. The measures included better recordkeeping and safeguards against graft. The legislation also contained a provision for the attachment of the estates of "foreign" debtors—that is, debtors who resided under a government other than that of North Carolina. The attachment measure pertained primarily to English merchants and others in the mother country who owed money to North Carolina creditors. Those "foreigners" sought to carry on business and commerce and to own property in the colony but without the restraints of its laws.

Conflict ultimately arose between the assembly and the royal government, which wanted the elimination of the attachment clause from the court law. When Josiah Martin arrived in the colony in 1771 to replace William Tryon (who had not openly challenged the attachment regulation) as governor, he brought with him orders from the British authorities to overrule the court law unless the attachment clause was removed. After the new governor disallowed the law in 1773, Caswell and Thomas Person, a western assemblyman, appealed to him directly to change his mind and accept the bill. Martin refused, however, arguing that laws of attachment should be separate from legislation pertaining to the courts and that in no other English colony was an attachment clause a component of the general court laws. The Colonial Council supported the governor.[10] Caswell and other supporters of the court bill maintained that attachment of estates "was necessary to [the colony's] commercial interests in proceedings against absconding debtors." Furthermore, even if the other colonies had their "foreign attachment laws separate from the general court laws, these laws had the sanction of the government and were as fixed and permanent as the court laws on which they necessarily depended."[11] The house insisted that "the right of foreign attachment is a right essential to every well regulated system of police, and is a security inseparable from traffic."[12]

The house and the council managed to reach a temporary compromise when they passed the court law, with the attachment clause, pending the approval of the king. The monarch, however, refused to authorize attachment and ordered Governor Martin to convene courts of oyer and terminer in lieu of the general courts. The governor appointed Caswell and Justice Maurice Moore Jr. to preside over these courts with Chief Justice Martin Howard. The house, however, refused to provide for the special courts. When it met in March 1774, the members informed the governor that they had the support of the populace in standing by the attachment clause. Martin tried once more for compromise, but the assembly would not reconsider. Because this conflict between the royal government and the colonial government could not be resolved, no courts convened in North Carolina again until after independence had been declared and the new state laws and courts went into effect.[13]

Like many important political leaders in early America, Caswell speculated extensively in land. The same ambition that motivated George Washington and other prominent men of the period inspired Caswell to believe in the acquisition of land as the means to wealth and social position. What one biographer, Ron Chernow, has written about Washington is equally true of Caswell. "For Washington," writes Chernow, "land speculation was the ideal vehicle for amassing riches, a way to invest in his own future and that of the country, mingling idealism and profit." Besides monetary value and social prestige, property bestowed a sense of self-determination and independence, a concept growing in Caswell and other Americans like him.[14] Although there is no evidence that he ever read John Locke's *Two Treatises of Government*, Caswell—like so many men of his time and place—exemplified Locke's philosophy that "property" represented more than land and wealth. For Locke and for them, a broad interpretation of property included a respect for man's equality, freedom and capacity to execute nature's law, to which they attributed their rights as free men. For early Americans, the ownership of property and the political rights and responsibilities of the individual were both natural and indivisible parts of their concept of liberty—a concept they sought to have reflected in the system under which they governed themselves. Their defense of this idea would ultimately play a large role in their seeking independence from the mother country.[15]

As was also the case with Washington and other ambitious Americans seeking to rise in wealth and social standing, Caswell's early career as a surveyor in his colony gave him the opportunity to investigate and evaluate new land for its future profitability. Caswell received his first grant of land in North Carolina in 1758. It comprised eighty-five acres on the north side of the Neuse River. He subsequently acquired thousands of acres—by purchase or grant—in Johnston, Dobbs, Orange, Cumberland, Carteret and Tryon Counties.[16] Contemporary records indicate that he was constantly engaged in the buying and selling of land. Colonial surveyors and land agents were sometimes guilty of charging illegal fees and quitrents and selling the same tracts more than once for their personal profit. One of North Carolina's most notorious land schemers was Francis Corbin, agent for the Lord Proprietor Earl Granville, in the so-called Granville District. The earl did not relinquish his share of North Carolina when the other Lords Proprietors signed over the colony to the royal government in 1729. Through his agents, Granville continued to sell land and collect rents until 1763, and Caswell worked as one of his surveyors. Because of Corbin's underhanded dealings, Granville finally dismissed him.[17]

Although Caswell obviously took advantage of his job as a surveyor for the colony to obtain lands of his own, he, unlike Corbin, was never accused of corruption in land allocation. The only known incident of criticism against him involved two land buyers referenced as

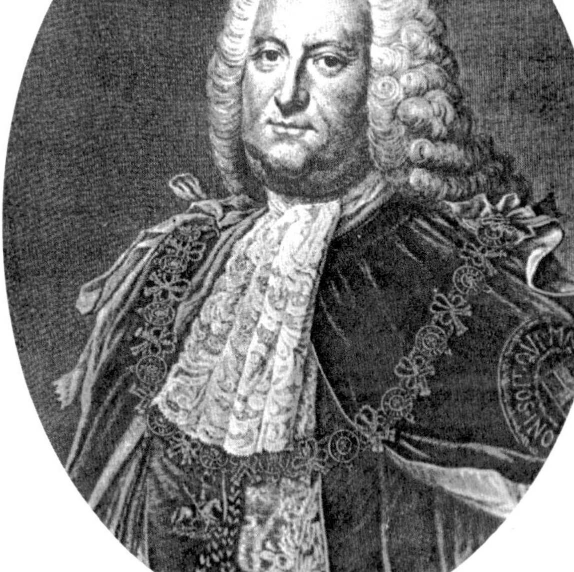

John Carteret, Earl Granville.

Moore and Becton, who claimed title to the same tract. Apparently, fees for surveying the land in question were charged more than once. A committee established in the assembly to investigate fraud in land transactions censored Caswell for failing to report that he had collected a fee for surveying the land for Becton while Moore had possession of it. In the dispute between the two claimants, the court decided in favor of Becton.[18]

Following the pattern of a number of large landowners and speculators in colonial America, Caswell had an interest in acquiring and exploiting western lands beyond the Appalachian Mountains. But the enthusiasm of such real estate entrepreneurs for western expansion and investment remained thwarted by the Proclamation of 1763, issued by the British government after its victory over the French in the French and Indian War. As a result of its triumph, Britain gained all the territory in North America between the mountains and the Mississippi River. The proclamation, however, reserved that region west of the mountains for the Indians, in large part to avoid warfare and land fraud between white settlers and the Native Americans.[19]

The authorities in London also hoped that restricting westward expansion would promote north–south migration in the colonies and thereby confine settlement to the eastern seaboard and maintain Americans' close ties to the mother country and its mercantile economy. Furthermore, such a settlement pattern might help serve as a "buffer against the Spanish in Louisiana and the remaining French in Canada." Despite the proclamation's prohibition against whites' settling, trading or entering into land transactions with Indians in the transmontane region, many speculators continued to press the royal government to make new treaties with the Indians that would allow for land grabs. Some of them ignored the act and attempted to negotiate directly with the Indians for tracts. The results were, according to historian Gordon S. Wood, "some of the most grandiose land schemes in modern history."[20]

Colonial North Carolina's most "grandiose" land schemer was Richard Henderson, who also served as an associate justice on the colony's superior court. While riding the circuit in western North Carolina, Henderson began to contemplate a plan for land purchase and settlement beyond the mountains, despite the royal government's proclamation prohibiting such incursions. In 1769, he sponsored a westward expedition, led by his friend the famed frontiersman Daniel Boone, to blaze a trail and investigate the possibility of land acquisition.

After leaving the bench, Henderson, in 1774, formed the Louisa Company, which included several prominent investors interested in profiting from western land sales. The company soon increased the number of members and renamed itself the Transylvania Company. The company signed an agreement with the Cherokee at Sycamore Shoals on the Watauga River. In that treaty, the Indians gave the company title to a tract that included present-day Kentucky and a large part of what is now Tennessee.[21]

On February 10, 1775, Governor Josiah Martin issued a public statement that Henderson's Transylvania enterprise was a clear violation of the Proclamation of 1763 and therefore a "lawless undertaking." He then proclaimed Henderson's negotiations with the Cherokee to be "illegal, null and void, to all intents and Purposes, and that all partakers therein will expose themselves to the severest Penalties." An earlier act passed by the Colonial Assembly imposed on anyone buying western Indian lands a "penalty of Twenty Pounds for every hundred acres so bargained for and purchased."[22]

Governor Martin suggested to William Legge, the Earl of Dartmouth, British secretary for the American colonies, that Henderson's land schemes in the West had inspired Caswell to launch a similar venture of his own beyond the mountains. The governor had come to "understand" that Henderson's idea "has given encouragement to another project of the like nature now carrying into execution . . . under the auspices of Mr. Richard Caswell, who is at the head of it." Martin further reported that his "information goes that [Caswell] and his Confederates (whose names I have not heard) are fitting out a vessel at New Bern to be sent up the Mississippi with chosen persons, to regulate with the Indians a purchase of lands lying to the westward of the Territory of Richard Henderson and his Company," and he had "no doubt if some effectual stop is not put to these daring usurpations that such Adventurers will possess themselves soon of all the Indian Country."[23] However, if Caswell had any such plans, they were not carried out. His attempts to speculate in land beyond the mountains did not take place until after the American Revolution.

And Governor Martin was not able to restrict or impose penalties on Henderson's operations, for his days as governor were numbered. Since the end of the French and Indian War, conflict between the British Parliament and the Crown's subjects over new trade and tax laws had grown. As the colonists increasingly moved toward revolution, Martin's influence and control in governing North Carolina weakened. Finally, powerless and fearing for his safety from the revolutionaries, he fled the colony in late May

1775 and took refuge on a British warship off the coast (see Chapter 3). With the colonial governor out of the way, Henderson and his partners persisted in their efforts to establish their Transylvania settlement. But the scheme folded when the new Continental Congress, meeting in Philadelphia, refused to recognize their project.[24]

In addition to his work and income from land surveying and acquisitions and his plantations, Caswell engaged in business, owning a tavern in Craven County and two stores in New Bern inherited from his father-in-law, William Herritage. At least one of his stores was destroyed by a horrific storm that struck the town in 1769, leveling fifty commercial buildings and residences.[25]

As was customary among wealthy eastern North Carolina planters, Caswell owned a large number of black slaves, though it is not certain how many he possessed at any one time. The United States census of 1790 (shortly after his death) reveals that his widow, Sarah, owned twenty-one slaves, and his son Winston owned six slaves.[26] In his will, probated in 1790, Caswell mentioned slaves bequeathed to other members of his family. To his grandson Richard William Caswell, he left "a Negro boy named Boson." To his grandson Richard Francis Mackilwean, he assigned "a Negro boy named Daniel." To his daughter Anna, he conveyed "Negroes Peter and his wife Barbara and Doll." Caswell also mentioned that he had once "purchased at the Vendue of the Estate of my son, Richard Caswell [deceased], . . . one Negro woman named Sarah, one Negro girl named Sall, one Negro boy named Charles, and one Negro boy named Jim." Those "said Negroes," he declared, "I leave the use of to my Daughter in Law, Mary Caswell, untill my niece, Sarah Caswell, her daughter, arrives at the age of eighteen years." In a codicil to his will, he assigned to his son Winston "Negroes Venus and Diamond."[27] Even during the Revolutionary War, Caswell continued to deal in human property. In April 1781, for example, he purchased from one Heritage [an in-law?] a slave named Tom for 150 pounds cash.[28] He never expressed any moral objection or ambiguity about slavery or found it incompatible with Americans' concept of liberty as expressed in the ideology of the Revolution. Caswell's slaveholdings definitely placed him among the wealthy elite of North Carolina in the late eighteenth century, for in the 1780s, "less than 1.5 percent of the adult white male population possessed twenty or more slaves in the typical eastern county." That figure compared with 6 percent in the Lowcountry of South Carolina and the Tidewater of Virginia.[29]

Thus, by the second half of the eighteenth century, Caswell had gained considerable experience and influence in the colonial government and established himself as a member of the eastern upper class of planters and large property owners. That eastern elite dominated society and wielded the largest share of power in the colony. But Caswell and his fellow members of the eastern gentry would soon find their economic and political control threatened by trouble brewing in the backcountry.

Chapter 2

Military Campaign in the Backcountry

In addition to his service in the colonial government, Caswell had acquired a degree of military experience. In 1754, he became captain of the militia company in Johnston County, for which he submitted annual reports for a number of years. After Dobbs County was formed from Johnston in 1758, he joined its militia, rising to command with the rank of colonel. (Dobbs became Lenoir County in 1791.) During the French and Indian War, Caswell did not engage in active combat, remaining occupied with his legislative service and land surveying.[1]

His first active military service came during the backcountry uprising known as the Regulator movement, or War of the Regulation. That revolt arose in the 1760s among folk, largely small farmers, in the interior of North Carolina who objected to corrupt local officials (appointed by the Colonial Assembly)—sheriffs, tax collectors, registrars, clerks of court, judges and land agents—who were collecting excessive and often illegal fees and taxes. The Regulators, as the organized backcountry dissenters called themselves, campaigned for significant change in local government. The struggle embodied elements of sectional and class conflict as residents of the western counties increasingly resented their lack of an effective voice in a colonial government controlled by a political power bloc in the east, dominated largely by wealthy planters and merchants—men of the same social and economic class as Richard Caswell. Evangelical Christianity embodied in the Protestant churches that dominated in the backcountry influenced the Regulators and helped unite them in moral opposition to what they

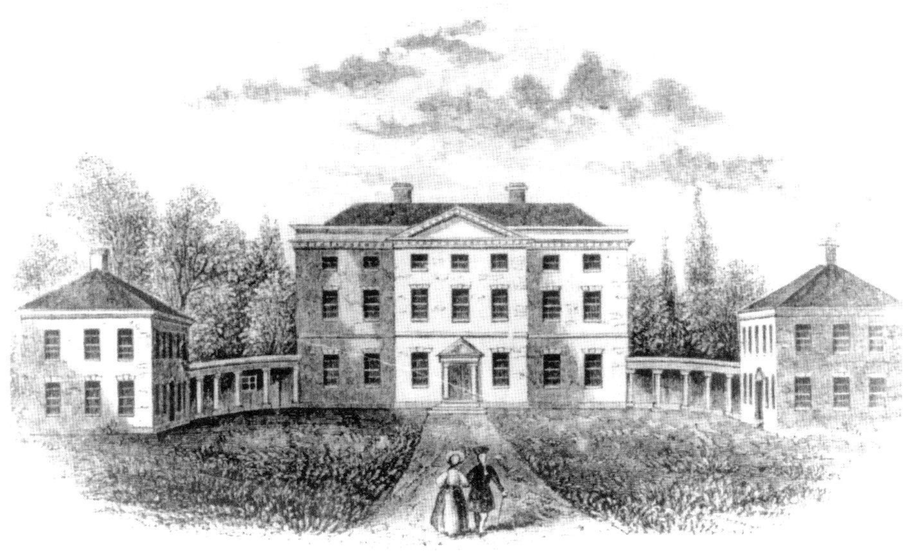

Governor's Palace in New Bern, built by Governor William Tryon.

considered an unjust and unethical system of government that failed to provide them relief from corrupt officials and to protect their property and their rights as citizens. Their protests went unheeded by the east-dominated assembly and ultimately led to armed conflict with the colonial authorities. The Regulators' chief leader was Herman Husband, a farmer from Sandy Creek in Orange County. Governor William Tryon, who replaced Arthur Dobbs in 1765, found himself having to deal with the growing discontent of the dissenters.[2]

Their frustration intensified when Tryon persuaded the assembly to locate a permanent capital at New Bern and build the Governor's Palace in that town. A new tax to pay for the grand edifice infuriated the farmers in the backcountry, most of whom would never see the governor or the palace. In March 1768, the Regulators, who used that name for the first time then, pledged to pay no more taxes or fees that were not specifically authorized by colonial law.

Up to a point, Tryon was sympathetic to the Regulators and their complaints. In December 1767, he called for better control over county offices to prevent corruption. The assembly responded by passing new regulations to prevent illegal collection of fees and other abuses by the clerks of court, as well as laws concerning the appointment and regulation of sheriffs and their duties. Despite those efforts at reform, conflict between the Regulators and local officials persisted.[3]

A volatile situation finally erupted in violence in the spring of 1768, when an Orange County sheriff seized a Regulator's horse, saddle and bridle as payment for his unpaid taxes. Outraged, a band of Regulators rode into Hillsborough, reclaimed their associate's property and fired guns into the house of Edmund Fanning, the most despised local official. Fanning, a well-educated native of New York, arrived in Orange County around 1760 and became register of deeds, judge of the superior court, a member of the

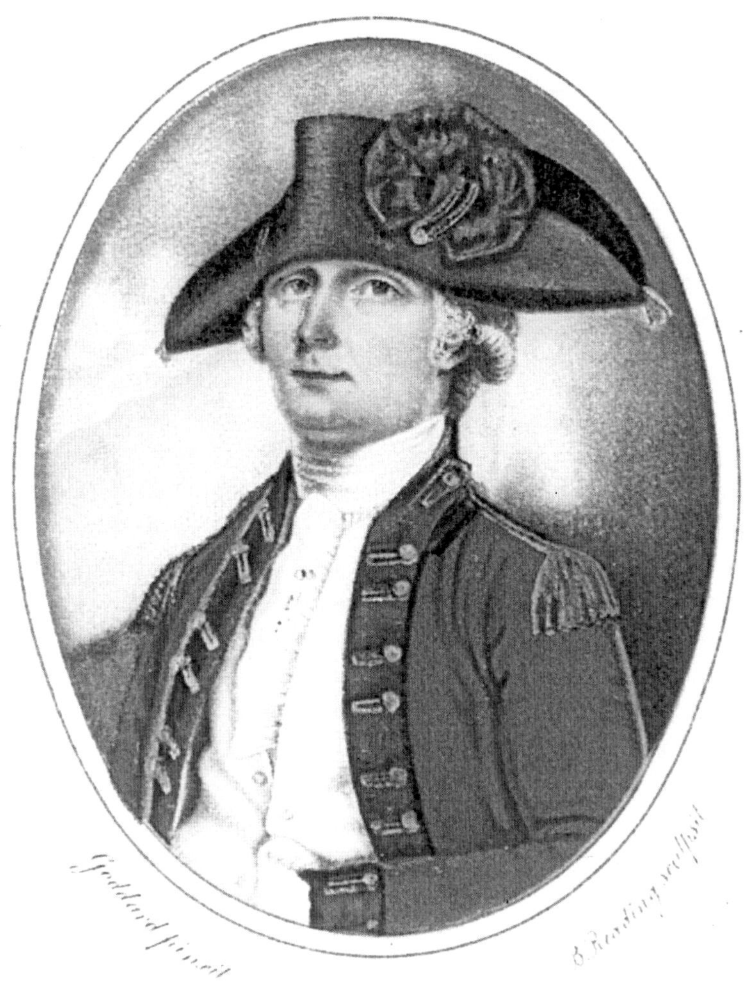

Edmund Fanning.

assembly and a militia colonel who used his positions to extort unauthorized fees from the folk in the interior of the colony. He treated most of them with contempt, and they—resentful of his arrogance and underhanded dealings—regarded him in the same way.

Following the incident in Hillsborough, Fanning organized an armed party that rode to Sandy Creek and arrested the Regulator leaders Herman Husband and William Butler. The two men were jailed in Hillsborough and charged with inciting a riot. A large number of armed men, many of whom were Regulators, then set out for Hillsborough to free Husband and Butler. Hearing of their approach, the sheriff released the two prisoners. When news of the conflict reached Tryon, he ordered that the Regulators disband, that lawful taxes be collected and that any official engaging in extortion be prosecuted. The Regulators immediately charged Fanning with extortion.

All three individuals—Husband, Butler and Fanning—were tried at the September 1768 session of the Orange County Superior Court. Husband and Butler faced charges of rioting. Husband was acquitted. Butler was convicted but, at the request of Tryon, received a pardon by the king. The court convicted Fanning of extortion, although he received no punishment other than a small fine, an outcome that infuriated the Regulators and increased their distrust of the courts. Fanning did resign his position as register of deeds. During the trial, Tryon led a contingent of militia to Hillsborough to protect the court in the event of trouble from the large number of Regulators who gathered nearby.[4]

Disappointed in the court ruling regarding Fanning, the Regulators turned to the assembly and the governor for further redress of their grievances. When the assembly met in 1769, a number of Regulators had been elected as members. Tryon, however, dissolved the assembly and called for new elections before their concerns were addressed. His reason was not directly related to the Regulators but rather to the quarrel between the colonial government and Parliament about taxation. Before adjourning, the assembly did resolve that any public official who charged illegal taxes or fees would suffer punishment.

Still angry at not having their demands addressed, the Regulators grew more restive, and in September 1770, they rioted at the Orange County Superior Court in Hillsborough. They broke up the court, assaulted several judges and lawyers, severely beat Fanning and wrecked his house, and terrorized some other residents who were not supportive of their cause.

When the assembly met in late 1770, the delegates and the governor intended to consider reforms to help farmers in the backcountry. But they heard rumors that Regulators were marching on New Bern. Instead of passing reforms, they refused to seat Herman Husband, who had been elected to the assembly, and had him jailed in New Bern for threatening the assembly and inciting riot. They also passed the Johnston Riot Act, which allowed colonial authorities to move court cases involving riots from one county to another. The act stipulated that anyone who did not respond to a court summons involving a riot case could be shot on sight as an outlaw and that the governor could use the militia to subdue rioters.[5]

Anxious to protect the capital and government from the Regulators he believed were marching toward New Bern, Tryon ordered Caswell to mobilize his Dobbs County militia to protect the town. The governor's November 20, 1770, dispatch to Caswell read:

> *From the reports generally prevailing in the Country that the Body of People who Stile themselves Regulators intend coming to Newbern during the sitting of the ensuing General Assembly to intimidate the Legislative Body, I think proper hereby to Command you to Assemble your Regiment on the first Notice you can get that the Insurgents are Assembling themselves and to Obstruct and oppose them in their progress through the Country to Newbern and even to repel Force with Force, but should you find it out of your Power to Collect a sufficient Number of Men in Time to effect that purpose, I must require you in Case they do come down to follow them to Newbern with all possible expedition with your whole Regiment in Order to protect the Legislature and to preserve the peace of the Government.*
>
> *It will be necessary for you to load as many Carriages with Provisions as will subsist your Men for fourteen Days at the rate of one pound and an half of Meat and one pound of Flour for each Man per Day.*[6]

Tryon also mobilized the Wake County militia under the command of Colonel John Hinton and the Johnston County militia under Colonel Needham Bryan. He alerted a number of other county militias, including Fanning's, to be prepared to campaign.

Caswell encamped his men at Kingston in position to defend New Bern. By late February, Tryon was still anticipating an onslaught on the capital by the Regulators. On the nineteenth of that month, he wrote to Caswell:

> *I am much obliged to you for the prudent Disposition you have made of your Men and the active Spirit you discover in these critical Times. The assurances you give of the Cheerful Resolution of your own and the*

> *Neighbouring Regiments in support of Government afford me the fullest assurance that We shall by their united aid be enabled to chastise the Insolence of any who shall dare to Offer any future Violence to the Persons or properties of his Majesty's Subjects in the Province.*

Tryon continued:

> *I hope to hear from you to Morrow by Noon whether the Insurgents are actually on their March or not. . . . When you are upon a Certainty that the Insurgents are not on their March you may dismiss your Men cautioning them to hold themselves in readiness to turn out again on the first Notice you may find it necessary to give them, which at the distance I am from you must be left discretionary with yourself.*[7]

On the following day, Caswell answered the governor that a force of Regulators had begun marching to New Bern but had halted upon receiving a letter from Herman Husband, who had been released from imprisonment, urging them to turn back. "[T]hey conclude[d]," reported Caswell, "to return, sayed their only view was to release him; And accordingly they did Disperse on Saturday last." The Regulators claimed that "13 waggons had crossed Haw River and 4 others were then on the South West side of the River ready to pass it." They reported to Colonel Hinton that their force comprised 2,200 men. Hinton, however, estimated that their number was fewer than 300, but well armed with small arms. "Colo. Hinton discharged his Men on Saturday," Caswell told the governor. "Colo. Bryan Discharged his on Sunday night, and in Obedience to your Excellys orders I have this Day Discharged the Dobbs Men."[8]

But that was not to be the end of Caswell's military campaign against the Regulators, who remained defiant. They pledged not to pay taxes and to kill Fanning. They threatened judges and clerks of court and vowed not to allow county courts to convene. In March 1771, the judges of the superior court at Hillsborough informed the governor that they would be unable to hold court without the protection of the militia. Upon receiving their request, Tryon felt compelled to resolve once and for all the trouble with the Regulators. Furthermore, he was soon to be transferred to New York as that colony's governor, and he wanted the conflict in backcountry North Carolina settled first. Consequently, he called up the militia. Among the regiments he summoned were Caswell's Dobbs County troops.[9]

On April 4, Tryon wrote to Caswell: "You will embody the Forces ordered to be raised from the Dobbs Regiment of Militia so as to March them the most convenient Route to Lieutenant Colonel William Bryans in Johnston County by the thirtieth of this month, they will then join the other Detachments Ordered to Rendezvous at that place when you will receive further Orders." Apparently, Caswell had notified Tryon that he lacked sufficient funds to recruit and equip his troops. Tryon answered him that "to Remedy the inconvenience you say you Labor under in the Recruiting Business for want of Money I send you a Draft on the Southern Treasurer for Six hundred pounds on account."[10]

Tryon and his force of about 1,100 militia, mostly from the east, arrived at Alamance Creek near Hillsborough on May 13. Camped nearby were 2,000 to 3,000 Regulators. In an attempt to flank the Regulators, another unit of militia, led by General Hugh Waddell, had marched toward Salisbury in Rowan County, but it had been halted by a large force of Regulators in the vicinity of Mecklenburg County. On May 16, Tryon's troops drew close to the Regulator camp.[11] Although it is not certain to what extent Caswell's troops participated in the fighting that ensued, in the militia's line of battle, three companies of Caswell's regiment occupied "the right wing of the 2d line," and one company stood "on the Left of the 2d line."[12]

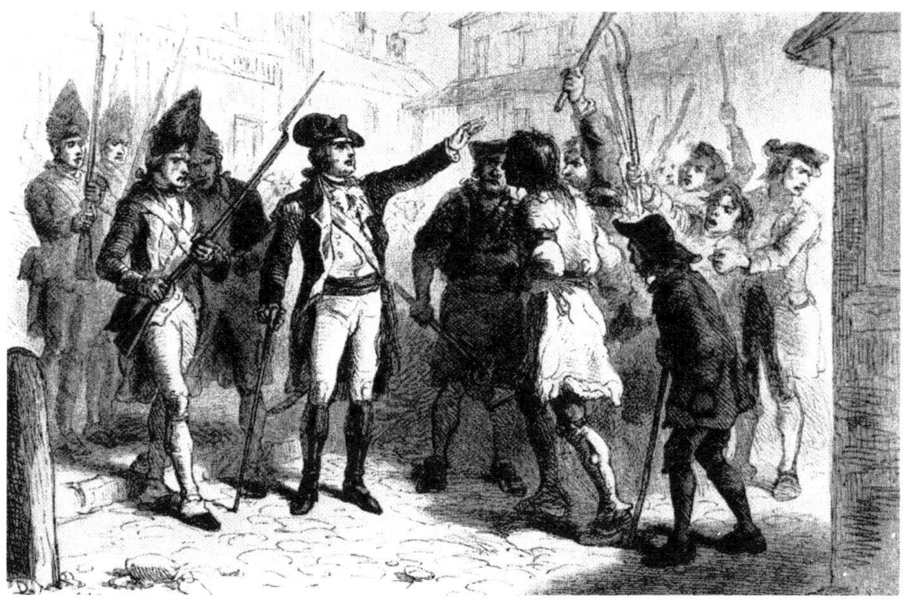

Governor Tryon confronts the Regulators.

As the two armed forces formed on the field, the Regulators dispatched three representatives to the governor asking for negotiations. Tryon refused to negotiate and demanded that the rebels lay down their arms, giving them one hour to decide. When the hour expired and the Regulators had not submitted, he ordered his men to open fire. At first, the Regulators seemed to be winning in the ensuing battle, but the militia soon gained the upper hand and scored a victory, with many of the Regulators fleeing the field. According to historian Marjoleine Kars, "Estimates of the dead and wounded vary; possibly as many as 20 Regulators were killed, along with 9 militiamen. Altogether, more than 150 men [on both sides] were wounded, many seriously." Tryon ordered the public execution of one of the Regulators who had been taken prisoner during the fighting. Beneath a tree with a noose around his neck, the rebel, young James Few, a carpenter, was twice offered a pardon by the governor if he would repent and renew his loyalty to the royal government. When Few refused both times, he was hanged. Kars notes, "Tryon later blamed his troops, claiming they had demanded such immediate 'public justice,' but more likely the governor and his officers wanted to intimidate the local population as well as those of their own soldiers who sympathized with the Regulators."[13]

Following the battle, the militia pursued the fleeing rebels and raided the settlements, farms and crops of many of the Piedmont inhabitants suspected of Regulator sympathies. The soldiers destroyed the houses, barns, fences and crops of rebel leaders James Hunter and Herman Husband. Caswell and his troops took part in those raids. Encamped on Husband's land on May 22, the regiment reported a roster of 162 rank-and-file soldiers, 2 drummers, 8 sergeants, 1 adjutant, 4 ensigns, 4 lieutenants, 4 captains, 1 major and Colonel Caswell.

Tryon soon proclaimed a pardon for those Regulators who would relinquish their arms and swear allegiance to the Crown. Excluded from the pardon were the leaders of the revolt. Tryon declared Herman Husband, William Butler, James Hunter and Rednap Howell to be outlaws and offered a substantial reward of money and land to anyone who would secure them dead or alive. About 6,400 Regulators took the loyalty oath and received a pardon. In June, a court of oyer and terminer in Hillsborough tried for treason 14 Regulators captured in battle. The court acquitted 2 and sentenced 12 to hang. Of the 12, 6 were hanged and 6 received pardons from the Crown on Tryon's recommendation. On June 20, with his immediate transfer to New York pressing, Tryon issued orders for the various regiments to march back to their respective counties and be discharged.[14]

Apparently, before disbanding entirely, Caswell's Dobbs County regiment took revenge on certain local persons of prominence who had been sympathetic to the Regulators. The *Virginia Gazette* of Williamsburg—which supported Tryon and denounced the Regulators—reported in August 1771:

> *We are advised from Dobbs County that since the Return of the Military Gentlemen of the County from the Expedition very spirited Measures have been pursued with a Number of Gentry who have been discovered to have held regulating Principles, and were ready to have joined the Regulators had they succeeded against the Provincial Forces. About ten of these People have been apprehended, tried by a Court Martial, and severely flogged at the Halberts* [a triangle of spearlike weapons erected for whipping].
>
> *That the Idle, the Dissolute, and Abandoned, who have Nothing to lose, should join in opposing Government, excites no Wonder, because, in the general Confusion, they have a chance to mend their Fortune, but the man of real Property who risks his Life on so precarious a Tenure must be a fool or a madman, or actuated by some malignant Principle of Revenge or Ambition, that degrades human Nature and prompts them to devour their own Species.*[15]

The *Gazette* did not specifically identify the prominent men of Dobbs who were tried and flogged. But it did note that one of them, "a Person of that County, of considerable Property, has thought proper to decamp rather than undergo the Discipline of the Halbert, which he might have submitted to, for being very deeply tinged with the regulating Notion."[16]

That some fellow members of Caswell's upper class sympathized with the Regulators and suffered public punishment for their opinions indicates that the movement was not entirely the result of sectional and class conflict between men of economic and social position in the east and the yeomanry in the backcountry. Retribution against them could also be interpreted as a caution to anyone in the east who might identify with the Regulators and their disruptive campaign. Whether Caswell himself ordered the court-martial and punishment of the Dobbs County gentry who were sympathetic to the Regulators is not clear. But as commander of the local militia, he must have played some role in authorizing the trial and sentences. The question also arises whether those punished were friends or associates or at least known to him.

There is, however, no ambiguity about his opposition to the Regulators and their cause. Like many pre-Revolutionary leaders in America, he originally professed and demonstrated obedience and allegiance to the British Parliament and king. In his career thus far, he had remained loyal to the royal governor and colonial government in North Carolina. The confidence and trust that Tryon placed in Caswell in the campaign against the Regulators and Caswell's role in that action are evidence of his loyalty to the Crown and its colonial governor, as well as his commitment to law and order and the protection of property, which he felt were threatened by the backcountry rebels.

The Regulator revolt, however, cannot be interpreted as direct defiance of king and Parliament and, as such, a type of prelude to the American Revolution. In fact, many of the Regulators would oppose war against Britain once the Revolution began, and some fought for the British. The Regulator movement, then, was not a revolt against Britain. It was an internal struggle against corrupt local officials and unfair and illegal taxes and fees. The rebellion can also be seen in large part as a sectional and class dispute between the poorer classes in the west and the wealthier and more politically powerful interests in the east, which dominated the Colonial Assembly. The Regulators' final objective was to secure for the folk of western North Carolina local autonomy and their political and individual rights. Ironically, the same colonial officials who had denied such reforms for the yeomanry in the backcountry soon demanded the same rights for themselves from the British Parliament. When denied those rights, they would not maintain their loyalty to the Crown, and among those severing ties to the royal government would be Richard Caswell.

Chapter 3

From Loyal Subject to Revolutionary

During the conflict with the Regulators, trouble was also swelling between the colonies, including North Carolina, and the government of Britain. As a result of the French and Indian War, Britain gained possession of all of North America east of the Mississippi River. The victory ended the conflict between Britain and France over territory on the continent and helped Britain grow as a world empire. But after the war, the royal government began to make greater demands on its American subjects by enforcing old and creating new regulations and laws to bring imperial organization to the colonies and to extract from them assistance in paying for the French and Indian War, for future defense and to support the empire. To achieve those aims, Britain began to enforce its trade laws with more diligence and to enact new duties or taxes on imports and exports. North Carolina and the other colonies came to resent and then openly oppose those imperial measures, and the relationship between the Crown and the colonies grew increasingly adversarial, ultimately erupting into war.

The new regulations that first angered Americans included the Proclamation of 1763, which denied them western settlement beyond the mountains; the Sugar Act of 1764, which particularly offended the New England colonies that imported molasses for rum manufacturing; and the Quartering Act of 1765, which required the colonies to provide living accommodations for British troops. North Carolina was not as upset by those new laws as were some of the other colonies because its settlers had not begun pressing beyond the mountains in large numbers, it did not

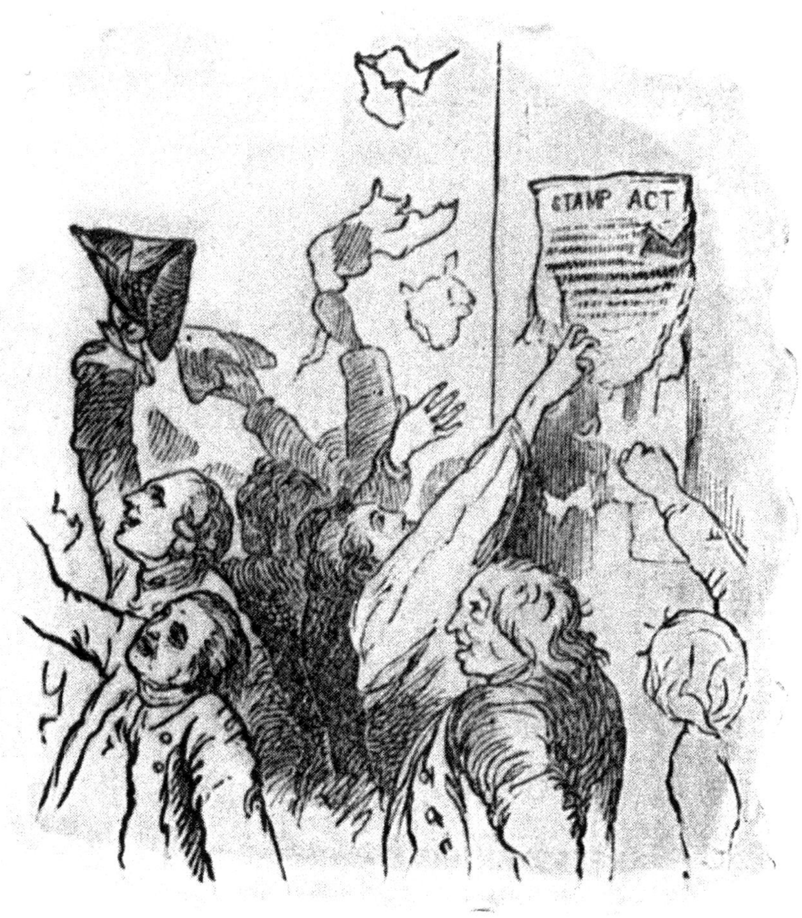

Residents of New Bern protest the Stamp Act.

import significant quantities of molasses and British troops did not occupy the colony.

But along with all the other colonies, the inhabitants of North Carolina responded with considerable outrage and opposition to the Stamp Act of 1765. That act required the use of stamps or stamped paper for all sorts documents, including legal documents, pamphlets, newspapers and even playing cards. The stamps indicated that a new tax had been paid on those items. The Americans' resentment was not assuaged by Parliament's promise to use the revenue from the stamps to defend the colonies. North Carolinians and their colonial neighbors raised a loud cry against the Stamp Act, calling it "taxation without representation!" They argued that because they were not directly represented in Parliament, that governing body back in London had no right to tax them. Only their local assemblies, in which they had representation, could tax them, they maintained.[1]

In North Carolina, the loudest protest against the Stamp Act occurred in the Cape Fear region. Five hundred residents met in Wilmington in October 1765 and forced the stamp agent there to resign. In the following month, a group of protestors prevented imported stamped paper from being unloaded at the port of Brunswick. Also at Brunswick, in February 1766, the British ship *Viper* seized two vessels because their clearance papers had not been stamped. A band of armed men, called the Sons of Liberty, broke into the customs office and reclaimed the papers of the two ships. They boarded the *Viper* and forced the captain to release the two vessels. A group also forced the customs collector to promise not to enforce the Stamp Act. He agreed to their demand and then resigned his position.[2]

Concerned about the opposition to the Stamp Act in the colonies, Parliament canceled the act in 1766. Nevertheless, at the same time, it passed the Declaratory Act, which proclaimed that—despite what Americans insisted—Parliament did indeed have the authority and right to tax the colonies. As if to prove their point, the British lawmakers passed revenue measures known as the Townshend Acts. That legislation placed duties on wine, tea, paper, glass and lead purchased in the colonies. The taxes were intended to pay the salaries of colonial governors and judges, who previously had been paid by the colonial assemblies. The North Carolina Assembly did not actively protest the Townshend Acts. Instead, in 1768, it sent a message to the king asking him to convince Parliament to repeal the duties. Again, the assembly asserted that it alone should determine what taxes North Carolinians paid. The king ignored the appeal.[3]

With the Townshend Acts remaining in effect, considerable opposition to their enforcement arose in New England, particularly at the port of Boston, where some merchants attempted to circumvent the duties, frequently engaging in smuggling that led the Royal Navy to confiscate some American vessels and cargo. To maintain its authority, enforce its laws and quell any possible uprising, the royal government landed additional troops in the Massachusetts port in late September 1768. As tension grew between the mother country and the Americans, the North Carolina Assembly voted for a "nonimportation association," which had been suggested by Virginia. Under the terms of the association, the member colonies agreed not to import any items on which duties had to be paid. The quarrel continued to swell between Bostonians' asserting their rights not to have taxes imposed on them and Parliament's insisting on its authority to levy such duties. The situation finally boiled over in the so-called Boston Massacre on March 5, 1770. In that event, redcoat soldiers fired on a belligerent mob in front of the customhouse, killing three people and wounding eight. Bostonians hardened in their opposition to British policy, and rumblings went through Parliament about treason.[4]

In an attempt at reconciliation—and also because the Townshend duties were not producing the anticipated revenue—Parliament revoked the duties on all the items specified in the act except tea. As a result, tempers cooled for a time on both sides, and importation resumed, although an undercurrent of resistance and suspicion continued to flow. Trouble arose again in 1772 over the royal government's pending trial of the men in Rhode Island accused of attacking and burning the revenue schooner *Gaspee*, which had been pursuing smugglers. The royal governor of Massachusetts, Thomas Hutchinson, further inflamed the local population when he announced that, in the future, his salary and the salaries of the colony's judges would come directly from the Crown. Many in Massachusetts saw those measures as usurpation of their rights and a weakening of their power over the colonial government. At the call of firebrand Samuel Adams of Boston, towns in Massachusetts formed Committees of Correspondence to communicate their opposition to British policies. They called on the other colonies to form similar committees. Virginia's House of Burgesses responded in March 1773 by appointing an eleven-man committee for intercolonial contact. Other colonies would soon follow with similar actions.

They would have much to consider following the Tea Act of May 10 and the Boston Tea Party of December 16, 1773. In addition to ending the tea duty in England and collecting it only in America, the Tea Act gave virtual control of the tea trade in the colonies to the East India Company by making it possible for the company to sell directly to retailers, thereby cutting the profits of American wholesalers, who would have to charge more for tea. When a consignment of tea arrived in Boston in late 1773, a group of protestors demanded that the transporting ships leave the harbor without unloading their cargo. Governor Hutchinson ordered the cargo taken off the vessels before they could depart the harbor. In response, a group of men disguised as Indians boarded the ships and threw the tea overboard.

The angered government in England concluded that the Bostonians had gone too far with their so-called tea party and cracked down on them by passing the Coercive Acts (March–June 1774). The first act closed the port of Boston to trade. The second declared that the king, not the colony's assembly, would appoint the members of the governor's council and that other officials and judges would be appointed or removed by the governor or nominated by him for the king's approval. It also prohibited the convening of town meetings except to elect town officials. The third act mandated that any royal official or soldier charged with a capital offense be tried in either England or Nova Scotia in order to avoid a biased jury in Massachusetts. The fourth act called for the quartering of troops in Boston. To ensure that these acts were carried out, the authorities in England appointed General Thomas Gage, who commanded British troops in North America, as governor of Massachusetts.[5]

Although the Coercive Acts (also known as the Intolerable Acts) were intended for Boston and Massachusetts, the other colonies identified with their plight, realizing that the same restrictions and mandates could be inflicted on them. In December 1773, the North Carolina Assembly had established its first Committee of Correspondence. Among the nine elected members was Richard Caswell. The others were John Harvey, Robert Howe, Cornelius Harnett, Edward Vail, William Hooper, John Ashe, Joseph Hewes and Samuel Johnston. Caswell was the only member from the middle region of eastern North Carolina, the other eight being from the Albemarle and Cape Fear regions.[6] The committee announced that it had the mission "to obtain early information of any acts of the British government in regard to the colonies, and to correspond with committees of other colonies as to their plans of resistance." It also insisted that all the colonies "ought to consider themselves interested in the cause of the town of Boston as the cause of America in general." Caswell and the other members vowed that they would "concur with and cooperate in such measures as may be concerted and agreed on by their sister colonies" and opined that to encourage and achieve "conformity and unanimity in the councils of America . . . a continental congress was absolutely necessary."[7]

On June 17, 1774, the Massachusetts legislature formally called for a congress of delegates from all the colonies to convene in September and recommended Philadelphia as the site. Upon hearing of the proposed meeting, Governor Josiah Martin refused to call the North Carolina Assembly into session in time for it to elect delegates to the Philadelphia gathering. "In that case," responded angry Speaker of the House John Harvey, "the people will hold a convention independent of the Governor." Other leaders also endorsed "a provincial congress independent of the governor." Local meetings throughout North Carolina elected delegates to attend the colony's First Provincial Congress, which met at New Bern in August. The delegates elected Harvey as moderator of the congress, which was attended by Caswell and other leading figures. The congress, which met for three days, denounced Parliament's tax policies, approved a boycott of trade with Britain, pledged support for Boston and Massachusetts and elected delegates to attend the First Continental Congress in Philadelphia in September. The delegates elected were William Hooper, Joseph Hewes and Caswell.[8]

Upon hearing that Caswell had been elected to attend the First Continental Congress, Governor Martin originally felt that because, in the past, Caswell had professed and demonstrated loyalty to the royal government, he would not be a strong supporter of the American opposition. "Richard Caswell," the governor wrote to the Earl of Dartmouth, secretary of state for the American colonies, on September 1, 1774, "has been appointed a delegate to the Continental Congress, but he disapproves of these measures in his heart, I am persuaded, and undertakes this office purely for the sake of maintaining his popularity on which he depends for continuance in the Treasurership which he has ever shown the best disposition to employ for the advantage of the government." Martin then considered Caswell to be "a man of the fairest and most unblemished character."[9] Within a year, however, Martin was painting a different portrait of Caswell, declaring that "he now shows himself to be the most active tool of sedition."[10]

On September 3, Caswell departed his Red House plantation for Philadelphia. He traveled with companions, including his son William, who kept a journal recording his observations about mileage, the countryside, accommodations and hardships of the journey. They reached Philadelphia on September 15, three days after the arrival of Hooper and Hewes. On the sixteenth, Caswell and his son attended a banquet honoring delegates to the Continental Congress, which event included a considerable amount of drinking. The delegates proposed thirty-two toasts during the evening. As recorded in William's journal, the subjects that they toasted give important insight into the topics most on their minds at the time. In particular, their proclamations indicated a strong residual loyalty to Great Britain and many of its leaders and the possibility of reconciliation with the mother country. Such sentiments, however, were matched by declarations of opposition to tyranny, the defense of liberty, constitutionality and sympathy and support for Boston in its recent trials. The toasts were recorded as:

> *1st the King. 2nd the Queen. 3 the Duke of Gloucester. 4th the Prince of Wales & Royal Family. 5 Perpetual union to the Colonies. 6 May the colonies faithfully execute what the Congress shall wisely resolve. 7 the much Injured Town of Boston and province of Massachusetts Bay. 8 May Great Britain be just and America free. 9 No Unconstitutional Standing armies 10. May the cloud that Hangs over Great Britain & the Colonies burst only on the Heads of the present Ministry 11 May every American hand Down to posterity, pure & untainted, the Liberty he has Derived from his Ancestors 12 May no man enjoy freedom that has not Spirit to Defend it. 13 May the persecuted Genius of Liberty find a lasting asylum in America. 14 May British Swords never be Drawn in defense of Tyranny. 15. the arts and manufactures of America. 16 Confusion to the authors of the Canady Bill* [see note]. *17 the Liberty of the press 18 the happy reconciliation between Great Britain & her Colonies on a Constitutional Ground 19 the virtuous few in both Houses of Parliament* [2]*0 the City of London. 21 Lord Chatham 22* [Charles Pratt] *Lord Cambden 23 Bishop* [of] *St. asaph* [see note] *24 Duke of Richm*[ond] *25 Sir* [Torn]*ville 26 the Marquis of Rockingham. 27 Mr* [Edmund] *Burke 28 General* [Henry Seymour] *Conway 29 Mr.* [John] *Dunning. 30 Mr* [John?] *Sawbridge 31st Doctor Franklin 32 Mr. Handcock.*[11]

Caswell took his seat in the Congress on September 17. It is not known what part he played in the debates or other business of the meeting. Silas Deane of Connecticut described Hooper, Caswell and Hewes in a letter to his wife. "The first," he wrote on September 23, "is a Bostonian bred, and educated at Cambridge College . . . ; a lawyer by profession, ingenious, polite, spirited, and tolerably eloquent. The other two are men of about forty, to appearance; of sedate and settled characters, well affected to the general Cause, but have not spoken as yet publicly."[12] Along with the other delegates, Caswell voted for the Suffolk Resolves, originally proposed by Massachusetts, which called for a boycott of trade with Britain and opposition to the Coercive Acts. But he received no committee appointments. Unlike Hooper, who was most active, he apparently did not become a significant voice at the Congress. In his journal, William Caswell spoke of enjoying the social life in the city, dining with other members or friends and shopping for clothes. He also mentioned visiting friends in New Jersey and relatives in Maryland before starting for home with his father after the Congress ended.[13]

Before it adjourned, the First Continental Congress approved the Continental Association, which prohibited all trade with Britain. It also authorized Committees of Safety in the counties and towns of the colonies to enforce the trade boycott, begin forming militias and promote and enforce loyalty to the American cause among their local populaces. In North Carolina, eighteen counties and four towns established Committees of Safety.[14] As time went on, these committees assumed more power as local civil governments. Governor Martin complained that they were "usurping some new authority every day. Executive, judicial or legislative, as the case may be," and their powers "soon became unlimited" in his view.[15]

The conflict between British authorities and the residents of Massachusetts continued to grow, and the sister colonies became increasingly sympathetic and concerned about their own relationships with the royal government. In North Carolina, Governor Martin—disgruntled with the Continental Congress, the trade embargo and the Committees of Safety—summoned the assembly into session in New Bern on April 4, 1775. At the same time, John Harvey called for North Carolina's Second Provincial Congress to convene. Most of the members of the Provincial Congress were also members of the assembly. Both bodies, then, met at the same time and elected Harvey Speaker of the assembly, thereby having him preside over the congress and the legislature simultaneously. The Provincial Congress asserted the people's right to assemble and petition the Crown about their grievances, and it approved the Continental Association established by the Continental Congress. Before adjourning, it authorized Harvey or his successor to call another Provincial Congress if necessary.

The members of the Provincial Congress who were not also members of the assembly were allowed to remain and participate in the discussions of the legislature. That action angered Martin, and he became further infuriated when the assembly approved the Continental Association, praised Caswell and the other two delegates to the Continental Congress and reelected them for any future meetings of that Congress. Annoyed and exasperated, Martin finally dissolved the assembly, which would be the last royal assembly to meet in North Carolina.[16]

Despite his efforts to arrest the growing opposition to royal authority in North Carolina, Martin soon found that events unfolding in Massachusetts were fast compelling a separation between him and many North Carolinians—including Caswell—who not too long before had been loyal subjects. In Massachusetts, General Gage had orders to seize any arms and ammunition that might be used by the colonials against British troops. Word had reached him that such munitions had been stored at Concord, a town northwest of Boston. On April 18, redcoats marched from Boston with the objective of seizing the weapons and ammunition at Concord and arresting rebel leaders. But the local minutemen (volunteer militia) received advance warning by riders from Boston, including the famed Paul Revere, that the British were on the way. Rebel leaders John Hancock and Samuel Adams were alerted to flee the area before they were captured. En route, the British soldiers fired on a contingent of minutemen at Lexington before moving on to Concord, where they found only a small quantity of supplies. On the way back to Boston, their extended columns were constantly attacked by a force of minutemen. By the time they reached the city, 275 British soldiers and 95 minutemen had been killed or wounded. Minutemen and militia surrounded Boston, and the British found themselves under siege. Thoughts of open revolt weighed on the minds of leaders on both sides. The Second Continental Congress then convened in Philadelphia on May 10, 1775, and called on the colonies to make preparations for war.[17]

As word of the conflict at Lexington and Concord spread throughout the colonies, tempers flared. In North Carolina, Committees of Safety spurred on efforts to organize and equip local troops, and talk of independence from the mother country was in the air. Those inhabitants who supported the American cause had come to be known as Whigs or Patriots. But not all North Carolinians favored a break with Britain. Many, called Loyalists or Tories, wanted to remain loyal to the Crown.

The Mecklenburg County Committee of Safety was swept with such a fervor of opposition that it passed the Mecklenburg Resolves on May 31, 1775. That document proclaimed that Mecklenburg County would not obey English law and would govern itself with "selectmen" until either the Provincial Congress established a permanent government or "the legislative body of Great Britain resign[ed] its unjust and arbitrary pretensions with respect to America."[18]

Around the time the Mecklenburg Resolves were issued, Governor Martin fled the capital at New Bern. Fearing for the safety of his family, he had already sent his wife and children to New York. In March, he had requested from General Gage weapons and ammunition to arm Loyalists for protection against attack by the Whigs. Locals' antagonism against the governor was stirred by rumors that he planned to arm slaves and use them in the event of a clash with the colonists. Seeing his power and authority slipping away and concerned for his own survival, Martin departed the capital and took refuge at Fort Johnston at the mouth of the Cape Fear River. There he continued to try to rally Loyalists until he learned that a force of minutemen was soon to attack the fort. He escaped just ahead of their arrival and found safety aboard the British sloop *Cruizer*.[19]

Meanwhile, Caswell, Hooper and Hewes had been dispatched back to Philadelphia to attend the Second Continental Congress. Caswell and Hewes left Halifax on April 30. En route at Petersburg, Virginia, they first heard the news of Lexington and Concord. From that point on, as they traveled with the Virginia delegation, they witnessed Patriots throughout Virginia and Maryland organizing into armed units. They arrived in Philadelphia on May 9. Hooper had been there for three weeks.[20] In Philadelphia, Caswell noted even greater military preparations. He described that activity in a letter to his son William and instructed him to encourage North Carolinians also to prepare for action. "Show them this letter," he wrote, "and tell them it will be a reflection on their Country to be behind their neighbors, that it is indispensably necessary for them to arm and form into a Company or Companies of Independents." He lectured William on how those companies should be organized and trained. "Receive no man but such as can be depended on at the same time reject no one who will not discredit the Company," he instructed.

As for Caswell himself, there is no doubt that by this time he had fully committed to the struggle for American liberty. "If I live to return [to North Carolina]," he declared, "I shall most cheerfully join any of my countrymen, even as a rank and file man, and . . . that or any other difficulties, I shall not shun whilst I have any blood in my veins, but freely offer it in support of the liberties of my Country." He instructed his son, "You, my dear boy, must become a soldier and risk your life in support of those invaluable blessings which once lost, posterity will never be able to regain."[21]

The Second Continental Congress had to consider the military situation around Boston. The British continued to fortify that port, and Massachusetts increased its militia surrounding the city. On June 14, the Congress established a Continental army and elected George Washington as commander, with orders to go to the Boston area and take charge of the colonial troops there. But before he arrived, a major battle took place in the hills overlooking the port city.

On June 17, British forces from Boston attempted to drive the Americans from Breed's Hill, adjacent to Bunker Hill, near Charlestown. In the ensuing Battle of Bunker Hill, as the conflict became known, the redcoats suffered heavy casualties before securing the objective. Washington arrived to take charge of the Continental army in Massachusetts on July 2, acknowledging—as did the British, the Continental Congress and people throughout the colonies—that the Americans' tenacious performance in the battle and subsequent encirclement of the British stronghold in Boston proved the depth of their commitment to the cause of independence.

With major fighting having occurred and a regular army in the field, the Continental Congress undertook the authority and responsibilities of a central government. It printed paper money to fund the army and established a committee for foreign negotiations. It called on the colonies to increase their preparations for war.[22] Caswell, Hooper and Hewes dispatched an appeal to Committees of Safety in North Carolina to follow the example of Massachusetts and other colonies and make a greater effort to prepare for war. "North Carolina alone remains an inactive spectator of this general defensive armament, supine and careless of her duty, it seems," they implored. "The crisis of America is not at a great distance."[23] Richard Cogdell, of the New Bern Committee of Safety, wrote to Caswell that "we have begun to put into Execution measures Similar to those you recommended." He also sent him a copy of the Mecklenburg Resolves, "inscribed" from a newspaper, noting that "the Mecklenburg Resolves exceeds all other Committees, or the Congress itself."[24]

To help rally the colony to the Patriot cause, Caswell returned to North Carolina in July, in time to spur on a Third Provincial Congress, which met at Hillsborough in August. According to historians David T. Morgan and William J. Schmidt, he had not distinguished himself at the Continental Congress, which adjourned on August 1. Hewes and especially Hooper were given important committee assignments, but Caswell was appointed only to a committee to consider Charles Lee, an English mercenary and veteran of the French and Indian War, for a commission in the Continental army. Morgan and Schmidt write that, "unlike his fellow delegates from North Carolina, Caswell received no assignment of significance." Instead, he was "virtually ignored in Congress." They speculate that "whether or not this had anything to do with his departure from Congress about June 28 cannot be said with certainty . . . but, in view of the fact that Caswell never returned to Congress, one might legitimately wonder if he disliked playing a subordinate role in Philadelphia."[25]

It is much more likely, however, that Caswell left Philadelphia early in order to undertake the task of organizing North Carolina's Third Provincial Congress. On July 8, Hewes reported to Samuel Johnston, convening the Third Provincial Congress, that "Caswell set off about ten days ago to meet the Assembly [Provincial Congress] which you say is expected on the 12th of this month. He carried most of the Resolves with him and will give you a particular account of our proceedings."[26]

Hooper and Hewes had joined Caswell by the time the Third Provincial Congress convened at Hillsborough. That body approved the measures of the Continental Congress. It raised two regiments for the new Continental army and organized six regiments of six hundred minutemen or militia each from the colony's six military districts. To govern North Carolina for the present, it would remain the chief body, with executive and judicial power vested in a Provincial Council, assisted by the district and local Committees of Safety. Finally, the Provincial Congress issued bills of credit as currency to fund the government and its defense efforts.[27]

On September 2, the Provincial Congress thanked Caswell, Hewes and Hooper for their service in the Continental Congress and elected them to serve in that body for another year. The delegates also appointed Caswell treasurer of the Southern District of North Carolina. Maintaining that he could not perform both tasks, Caswell resigned his position in the Continental Congress. The Provincial Congress then elected John Penn to replace him at Philadelphia. In contrast to Hooper, Hewes and Caswell, Penn "was no tidewater aristocrat." A native of Virginia, he studied law before moving to Granville County, North Carolina. "As a hinterlander

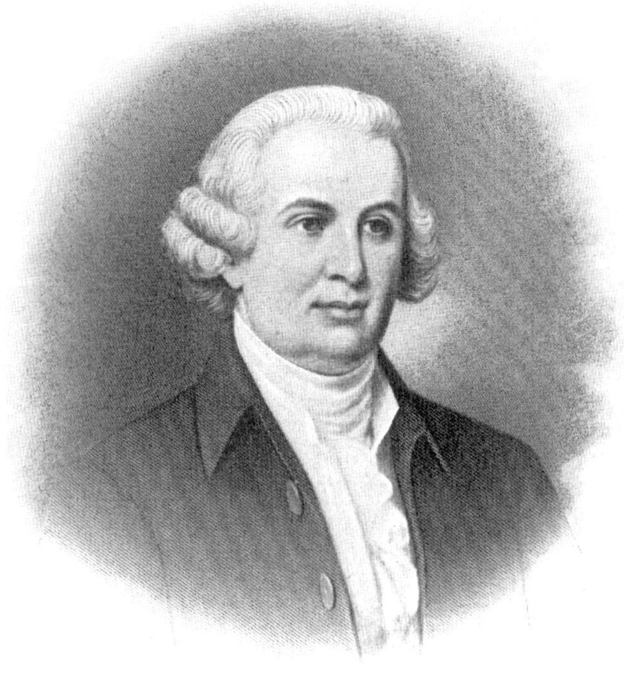

William Hooper.

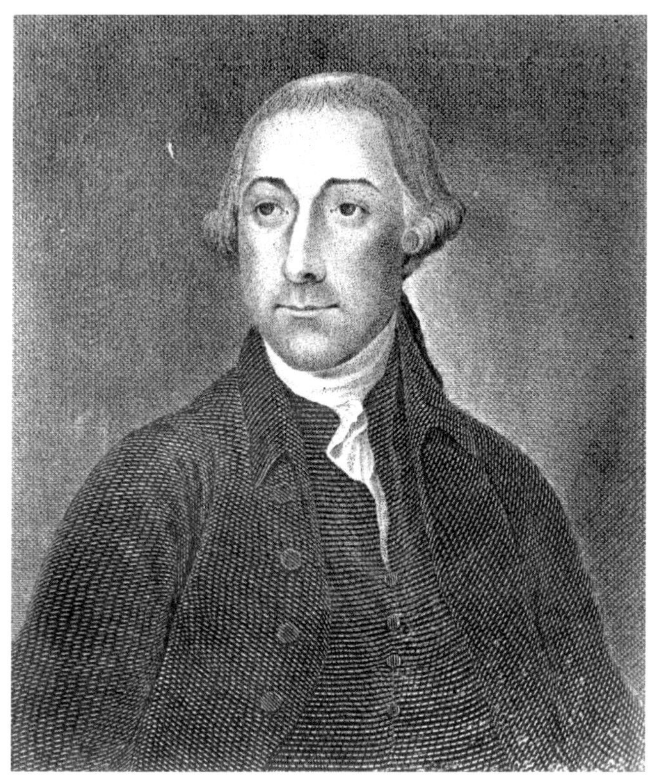

Joseph Hewes.

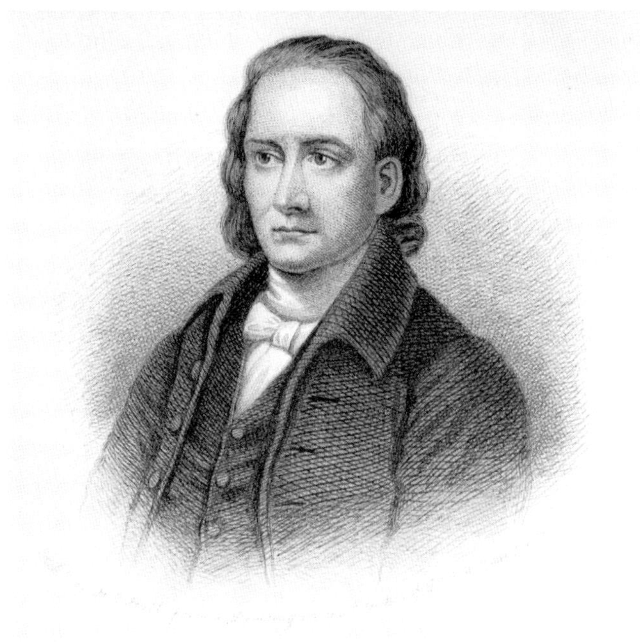

John Penn.

considered sympathetic to democratic ideals," write Morgan and Schmidt, "Penn was chosen to replace Caswell in an attempt to allay the east-west sectional antagonism which cropped up in the Third Provincial Congress." Penn would achieve fame as one of North Carolina's three signers of the Declaration of Independence.[28]

From his exile off Cape Fear, Governor Martin denounced the Third Provincial Congress and specifically Caswell's role in creating that congress and as a delegate to Philadelphia. On August 15, he issued a proclamation to North Carolinians who were still loyal to the Crown (of whom he conjectured there were many) attacking the Provincial Congress and Caswell in particular. He announced, "I do hereby most especially admonish His Majesty's faithful Subjects in this Colony, that the holding what is called a Provincial Convention at Hillsborough . . . is calculated to extend more widely the traiterous and rebellious designs of the Enemies of His Majesty and His Government, and the Constitution of this Province, and particularly to influence, intimidate and seduce His Majestys Loyal and Faithful Subjects." The man most responsible for such "rebellious designs" was none other than "a certain Richard Caswell, one of the three Persons deputed by a former illegal Convention in this Colony to attend a Congress no less illegal at Philadelphia [and who] is sent an Emissary from that Assembly . . . to forward and superintend this meeting at Hillsborough and to enflame it with the fatal example of the Philadelphia Congress, a part which he has entered upon with the most active zeal . . . thus exhibiting himself to the world a monstrous engine of double treason against his own conscience and against His King and Country." Martin also resented Caswell's reaction to his flight from the colonial capital. "At New Bern I am credibly informed that he had the insolence to reprehend the Committee of that little Town, for suffering me to remove from thence," whined the former governor.[29]

Still, at this time the colonies had not called for an open break with the mother country and even had held out the possibility of reconciliation in a document known as the Olive Branch Petition. King George III, however, rejected the petition and declared the colonies in rebellion. By late 1775, fighting had already broken out between the Americans and the British army in the North: at Lexington and Concord, Bunker Hill and Fort Ticonderoga on Lake Champlain and during an American expedition into Quebec, Canada.[30] With the possibility of further armed conflict looming, Caswell wrote from Newington to his son William, commanding the New Bern militia, to remain steadfast and be prepared to fight for the American cause. "I hope my Dear Child," he told William on February 8, 1776,

> *the Virtuous cause you are engaged in and the hope you have of giving the little Assistance in your power to the relief of your Country, and as far as your power extends, will Stimulate you to put up with Hardships, Fatigues & inconveniences which others may shudder at, to ward off that Slavery which is Attempted to put the present, as well as the future, generation under in this once happy Land. Don't mistake me when I say the dissatisfaction of others ought not to be a rule for you, nor think that I would wish you to be one Moment in a Service your Conscience does Not tell you it is your duty to Attend and even Sacrifice that life which I have been an instrument in the Hands of your Maker of giving you. You know I would not wish you to remain a day longer from me or those of your Family to whom you are very dear if I did not think your own, mine & Our Country's Honor & Welfare required it.*[31]

At that same time, the conflict was, indeed, moving southward, and North Carolina soon became a major target of the British.

Although Governor Josiah Martin had taken refuge offshore aboard the *Cruizer*, he continued to make plans to suppress the American rebels and capture the important port of Charleston, South Carolina, which might prove key to gaining control over the southern colonies. He informed British officials that he believed he could recruit in North Carolina at least three thousand troops to fight for the Crown. That army of Loyalists would join with British regulars in a southern campaign.

The authorities in England adopted some of Martin's suggestions and decided in early 1776 to have two fleets transport armies to the Cape Fear River. One army, under the command of General Henry Clinton, would sail from Boston. The other, commanded by Lord Charles Cornwallis, would depart from Ireland. The loyal North Carolina troops raised by Martin would march toward Brunswick and Wilmington on the Cape Fear and join the two armies of redcoats. The combined force would then proceed to capture Charleston.

Upon receiving confirmation of this British strategy, Martin launched his efforts to recruit among North Carolinians. He called on loyal subjects to rise against the rebels and authorized the Loyalist leaders in several counties to organize and equip militia and march to Brunswick by February 15, when the fleets carrying the soldiers of Clinton and Cornwallis should have arrived.

Martin considered the most important component of this mobilization to be the enlistment of the Highland Scots of Cumberland County. Numbers of Scots had settled along the Cape Fear River, particularly after Scottish leader Charles Edward Stuart ("Bonnie Prince Charlie") led them in revolt against England, which ended in their defeat at the Battle of Culloden in 1746. The Crown then granted them land in North Carolina once they had taken an oath of allegiance. Thereafter, they remained loyal to the king and established themselves primarily around Cross Creek (present-day Fayetteville).

But Martin also hoped to gather recruits for his expedition from the Regulators in the backcountry. Since their defeat at the Battle of Alamance in 1771, many of the Regulators and their sympathizers had retained their resentment against the dominant political powers in the east. Martin felt that because the present rebellion against the British government was primarily the work of the eastern power bloc, a sizable number of people in the interior could be called on to support the British campaign to suppress an uprising.[32]

From Boston, General Gage dispatched two officers to North Carolina to organize and lead the loyal troops in the expedition to the coast: Lieutenant Colonel Donald MacDonald (soon promoted to brigadier general of militia) and his second in command, Captain Donald McLeod (soon promoted to lieutenant colonel of militia). They summoned the Scots and backcountry volunteers to Cross Creek and Cross Hill in Cumberland County for arming and training. Ultimately, the large number of Regulators and other backcountry Loyalists of whom Martin had high hopes of support failed to participate in the campaign. Many remained at home; some marching to the rendezvous were driven back by Whigs, and others became disaffected and left Cross Creek to return to the interior. The Scots would make up the largest portion of the Tory army, which on February 15 had about 1,400 men, of whom about 520 had firearms. A number were armed with claymores, traditional Highland swords.[33]

The Whigs in eastern North Carolina quickly responded to the Loyalist gathering in Cumberland County. Two Continental regiments, commanded by Colonel James Moore of New Hanover County and Colonel Robert Howe of Brunswick County, began moving toward Cross Creek. Moore served as the senior officer for the expedition. Units of militia and minutemen also mobilized. Colonel Alexander Lillington, the militia commander of the Wilmington District, called up his command. The New Bern Committee of Safety also ordered its district's militia and minutemen, under Colonel Caswell, to march in support of Moore. Caswell's unit had artillery, and he was authorized to procure supplies and wagons en route to Cross Creek.[34]

MacDonald realized the urgency of beginning his movement as Moore's contingent of two thousand men drew within seven miles of Cross Creek and established fortifications at the bridge over Rockfish Creek, thereby blocking MacDonald's most direct route to the coast. Farquard Campbell, a captured Loyalist paroled by the Patriots, soon arrived in MacDonald's camp with the additional news "that Richard Caswell and a force of six hundred men [were] on the march to join Moore."[35]

Seeing the necessity of moving before Moore was reinforced, MacDonald set his men on the march on February 18. Drawing near Moore's defenses at Rockfish Creek, he sent word to Moore that he and his men faced severe punishment from the Crown if they did not surrender. The Whigs, however, stood their ground. MacDonald, aware that he was outnumbered and losing troops to desertion, then decided to bypass Moore's defenses before more Patriot troops arrived. He moved his Tories back to a point near Cross Creek, where they boarded boats, crossed the Cape Fear River and resumed their march.

Moore quickly saw that he had been outflanked and ordered some of his troops to occupy Cross Creek to deny the Loyalists a point for retreat or return. Knowing that Caswell was on his way, he ordered him to change direction and move to a defensive position at Corbett's Ferry on the Black River. Moore meanwhile moved to Elizabethtown to block the main road to Wilmington. Caswell's troops took up a position at the ferry, where their equipment included the two light artillery pieces "Old Mother Covington and her daughter." But MacDonald managed to evade Caswell's opposition by crossing upstream from the ferry and pressing on toward the coast.

Realizing that he had been outflanked, Caswell followed Moore's contingency orders and raced to Moore's Creek Bridge to get in front of MacDonald's column. There, Caswell's eight hundred soldiers were joined by Colonel Lillington and his battalion of minutemen from Wilmington. The narrow bridge, located about seventeen miles from Wilmington, stood at a high elevation and on a sandbar. The creek itself flowed through land owned by the widow Elizabeth Moore, from whom it took its name. It was fifty feet wide and five feet deep at the bridge. It emptied into the Black River, which flowed into the Cape Fear about ten miles away. The site proved excellent for an ambush by Caswell and Lillington. Caswell's men entrenched on the west side of the creek, with their backs to the stream, while Lillington's soldiers occupied the east side.[36]

When MacDonald's column drew to within a few miles of Moore's Creek Bridge, the Tory leader learned from his scouts that Caswell had arrived there first. He dispatched a messenger to Caswell's camp to demand a surrender. But MacDonald did not really believe that Caswell would surrender. The messenger's true mission was to serve as a spy, and he reported that Caswell

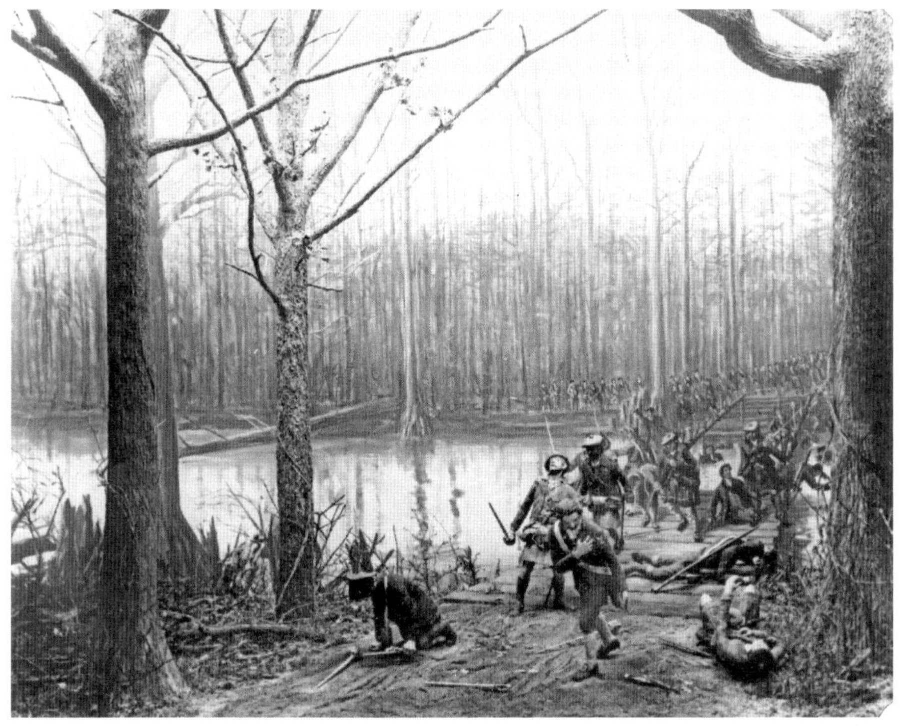

A diorama depicting the Battle of Moore's Creek Bridge.

was in the vulnerable position of having his back to the creek. MacDonald therefore decided to attack at daybreak the next day. However, he had taken ill and turned over command of the assault to his subordinate, McLeod.

Just before dawn, the Loyalists attacked what they thought was Caswell's camp, where fires continued to burn. But during the night, Caswell had moved his men across the creek, where they joined Lillington's troops. McLeod now faced the difficulty of attacking across the bridge.[37]

The crudely constructed wooden bridge made it particularly difficult for the Loyalists to cross in force. The Patriots had removed the planks and greased the logs that anchored them. McLeod and Campbell, leading their men across, were both killed. Volleys from "Old Mother Covington and her daughter" and the Whigs' muskets cut down the Tories, a number of whom fell into the deep water at the bridge. The battle was over in minutes. Only two of Caswell's and Lillington's men were wounded, though one subsequently died of his injury. At least thirty of the Loyalists were killed outright, and probably even more died later of wounds. The survivors, including MacDonald, fled in full retreat.

Meanwhile, Colonel James Moore had joined Caswell and Lillington. Assuming overall command, he ordered a pursuit of the enemy. MacDonald was soon captured and jailed, first at New Bern and then at Halifax. The Whigs quickly surrounded the main body of retreating Tories. About 850 of the rank-and-file soldiers captured received paroles. But their officers—numbering at least 30—were jailed at Halifax along with General MacDonald and the famed Flora MacDonald's husband, Captain Allan MacDonald. The paroled Loyalists who returned to their homes and communities found themselves in conflict, often violent, with their Whig neighbors. Some had their property confiscated after a state government was formed, and a number fled to Nova Scotia and other parts of Canada.[38]

The battle might have ended differently if the forces of Clinton and Cornwallis had arrived on time as planned to help resist the Whigs. But the two fleets did not fully assemble at Cape Fear until May 3, 1776. Some British landing parties came ashore and raided and plundered—including burning a number of plantation houses—along the river. Fearing a British invasion, Moore mobilized his troops, including Caswell's New Bern contingent, to defend coastal North Carolina. But the British raids amounted to little, and the fleets soon weighed anchor and moved on to attack Charleston, which they failed to capture.[39]

Caswell's role in the Battle of Moore's Creek Bridge did much to bolster his reputation as a leader. He performed well in commanding troops in the campaign. His decision to deceive the enemy by moving his men across the creek under cover of darkness demonstrated a certain tactical acumen and helped to secure victory. But historian Hugh F. Rankin has written that the "victory was to eventually end in controversy, albeit of a local nature. The point of argument was, Who had been in command at Moore's Creek Bridge, Lillington or Caswell?" This question was argued for some years by proponents of both men. "From the available evidence," writes Rankin, "there seems little doubt that Caswell was the commander in the field, but the argument fails when the consequences are fully weighed." He maintains that "the real hero of the campaign was James Moore, although he was not a participant in the ultimate battle. It was Moore who, with all the finesse of a master chess player, maneuvered his troops in such a fashion as to effectively seal off the loyalists from their objective and force them to do battle on ground of his choosing."[40] But at the Continental Congress in Philadelphia in March, "some letters and Papers from N Carolina were read giving an Acot. of the Defeat of the Tories by Col. Caswell."[41] When North Carolina's Fourth Provincial Congress convened at Halifax in April, it resolved "that the thanks of this Congress be given to Colonel Richard Caswell, and the brave officers and men under his command, for the very essential service by them rendered this country at the battle of Moore's Creek."[42]

The Fourth Provincial Congress marked a point of no return for North Carolina as the colony moved toward independence. The Battle of Moore's Creek Bridge had been the first major clash of arms in North Carolina. The Whig victory halted an invasion by British regulars, and there would be no successful invasion until 1780, when the redcoats returned to the Carolinas. But blood had been shed in North Carolina and, along with it, any hopes of reconciliation. When the delegates to the Fourth Provincial Congress gathered in Halifax on April 4, 1776, a cry for independence was almost certain to be the result. Indeed, on April 12, they approved the Halifax Resolves, which instructed North Carolina's delegates to the Continental Congress to vote—in cooperation with delegates from the other colonies—for independence from Britain.

When North Carolina's delegation arrived in Philadelphia, it presented to the congress its instructions from the Provincial Congress. In the meantime, Virginia's Provincial Congress had authorized its delegates to Philadelphia to call for independence, which the other delegates endorsed. The Continental Congress then urged the colonies to establish new state governments, and it formed a committee to establish a confederation. Soon, New Hampshire, South Carolina and Virginia began writing state constitutions.[43]

Prior to adjourning on May 15, North Carolina's Fourth Provincial Congress considered adopting "a temporary civil constitution" to specify a central government for North Carolina, but it decided to postpone drafting such a document. Instead, the congress established a Council of Safety, which included Caswell and eight other men, to govern the emerging state in continuous session until a state constitution could be written. The Provincial Council, created by the Third Provincial Congress, was abolished along with the six district Committees of Safety, although the local Committees of Safety remained in operation. In addition to serving as a central government for North Carolina, the Council of Safety was to procure troops, money and supplies and ensure the population's loyalty to the Patriot cause. Challenges that confronted the Council of Safety included dealing with Loyalists and Regulators, the threat of British attack on the coast and attacks by Cherokee Indians on the frontier. Before the Halifax congress disbanded, Caswell served on several committees, reported North Carolina's expenses to the Continental Congress and helped prepare cost projections for future military preparations.[44]

At the Continental Congress on June 7, 1776, Virginia's Richard Henry Lee rose and proposed "that these United Colonies are and of right ought to be free and independent States." The Congress adopted his resolution on July 2 and, two days later, approved the Declaration of Independence, written largely by Thomas Jefferson. North Carolina's signers of the declaration were William Hooper, Joseph Hewes and John Penn (who had replaced Caswell in Philadelphia). News of the "immortal document" reached the North Carolina Council of Safety, meeting at Halifax, on July 22. It quickly passed a resolution that Americans "were absolved from all Allegiance to the British Crown." On August 9, the Council of Safety called for an election to be held on October 15 for the voters to choose delegates to a Fifth Provincial Congress, to convene at Halifax. The mission of the fifth congress was to draft North Carolina's first state constitution. The council urged the voters "to pay close attention" in choosing their delegates because those representatives were "to form a Constitution for this state," which would be "the Corner Stone of all Law, so it ought to be fixed and Permanent, and that according as it is well or ill Ordered it must tend in the first degree to promote the happiness or Misery of the State."[45]

On November 12, 1776, the Fifth Provincial Congress met at Halifax. The delegates unanimously elected Caswell as president of the congress and appointed a committee to draft "a Bill of Rights and Form a Constitution." Caswell chaired the committee. The delegates read and debated extensively the constitution and the bill of rights, although no record of their discussion has survived. They approved the bill, known as the Declaration of Rights, on December 17 and the constitution on the following day. The two documents were then printed and distributed throughout North Carolina, but they were not presented to the voters for popular ratification. The Declaration of Rights contained twenty-five articles that specified the individual rights of North Carolinians that had to be observed by the government. The North Carolina Constitution created three branches of state government: executive, legislative and judicial. The document deliberately limited the authority of the governor, placing the largest political power in the General Assembly. The legislature would elect the governor and appoint all members of the executive branch and judges. All actions taken by the governors—who could serve one-year terms and only three terms in a six-year period—had to be approved by the Council of State. Those delegates who wrote the constitution reflected a general desire of many North Carolinians to restrict the chief executive's powers because of past difficulties with royal governors. The drafters of the document also included such conservative measures as property qualifications for holding state offices and a stipulation that only those voters who owned fifty acres of land could vote for the state senate.[46]

The majority of the delegates who had served in North Carolina's five Provincial Congresses, including Caswell, had also served in the Colonial Assemblies. According to one historian, Robert L. Ganyard, they were "men of property who represented the conservative point of view." When county elections selected delegates to participate in the writing of the state constitution, heated arguments had arisen between "radicals" and "conservatives" about how democratic the new constitution should be. "Yet," maintains Ganyard, "when the convention assembled, a spirit of moderation prevailed, the committee appointed to draft the constitution was dominated by 'conservatives' and 'moderates,' and the constitution which it produced . . . was an essentially conservative document." He further asserts that "the evidence suggests that in North Carolina, as in most other states, the proponents of democracy, while active and not without influence, were nevertheless insufficiently powerful and too poorly organized to be the center of the Revolutionary movement or to represent its principal thrust."[47]

However, it is possible to exaggerate the "conservatism" of Caswell and the other leaders of Revolutionary North Carolina. According to historian Milton Ready, the convention writing the state's first constitution was "almost evenly divided between radicals and conservatives." Furthermore, the drafting of the Declaration of Rights—which preceded the writing of the constitution itself and expanded the convention's concept of democracy and individual liberties—helped ensure that the rights of the people were not overshadowed by laws for the protection of property and status quo principles of government. The declaration was strongly supported by the "radicals" in the backcountry. Ready maintains that "North Carolina's Revolutionary constitution reflected the ascendancy of radical Whiggery, or popular democracy, and a movement away from the more conservative ideas of men such as William Hooper and Samuel Johnston, the initial leaders of the rebellion against England." He gives much of the credit for writing the document to Caswell and Thomas Jones, lawyer and former colonial official from Chowan County, "both of whom represented the shift away from conservative and to increasingly popular forms of democracy."[48]

Even if Caswell is construed as a "conservative" or perhaps a "moderate" (as some historians might wish to call him) in constitution making, he displayed no restraint or even ambiguity in his support for the rising military struggle for American independence. The Fifth Provincial Congress quickly chose him to lead North Carolina in the looming armed conflict with the British.

Chapter 4

Governor in the Struggle for Independence

Because a governor could not be elected until the General Assembly met, the Provincial Congress, which closed on December 23, appointed Caswell to serve as governor of the new state until the legislature convened. Along with other officials of the executive branch, he took the oath of office in New Bern in January 1777. The *Virginia Gazette* described his inauguration in a report from New Bern on January 14:

> *On Friday last, his Excellency Richard Caswell, Esqr. Governor of this State, arrived here. He was met about six miles from town by about thirty gentlemen on horseback, who accompanied him to New Bern, the bells ringing as soon as he entered the town. Being conducted to Mr. Edward Wrenford's tavern, where a handsome collation was prepared, he received from the Continental officers and soldiers (drawn up for the purpose) a salute with small arms; the fort,* Pennsylvania Farmer, *and the other vessels in the harbour, fired many guns, under a display of the colours of the United States, and in the evening the town was highly illuminated.*
>
> *On Monday the 13th instant the inhabitants assembled, and waited upon his Excellency with a congratulatory address.*[1]

In their flowery address to Caswell, the inhabitants of New Bern declared that,

> *uninfluenced by private ambition and sordid interest, you have ever pursued the good of your country. Mankind have been taught, by your example, that the love of liberty, and a steady perseverance in acts of private and public virtue, are the surest ways to preferment, and the best title to the honours of a free State. We have not a doubt, therefore, but that your Excellency's endeavours in your important station will give full satisfaction to the most sanguine expectations of the public.*

Caswell thanked the crowd for its "congratulations on my appointment to the supreme command of this State" and declared:

> *My election to that important office, by the unanimous suffrages of the representatives of a free people, unsolicited by me, I consider as the highest honour I could receive, and shall ever think it my duty to pursue every measure in my power for the benefit and prosperity of this State, and to promote the happiness and safety of its inhabitants, and in doing which, if I am so happy as to give satisfaction to the public, my utmost wishes will be answered.*[2]

The General Assembly held its first session in New Bern on April 7, 1777, and on the eighteenth of that month, it reelected Caswell as governor. During his terms as war governor, Caswell generally resided at his Newington plantation, and the Council of State and the General Assembly frequently met in Kingston. Upon taking up his office, Caswell found that he faced myriad difficulties as the new state's chief executive. Perhaps the most pressing of his problems was keeping state troops in the field in the cause of independence.

The Continental Congress persistently requested soldiers from the states to serve in the Continental Line, though none of the states ever filled its quota completely. Soldiers' pay in paper scrip was low and virtually worthless. A large part of the population were Loyalists unwilling to fight against the Crown, and other men were reluctant to leave home and family to fight in a war that might not prove victorious for the United States. Yet North Carolina supplied ten regiments—6,086 to 7,663 soldiers—to the Continental Line in the Revolution. The largest number of North Carolinians served in the militia, which required service from all males who were at least sixteen years old. The militia in general was not as competent a fighting force as the regular army, although 10,000 North Carolinians served in its ranks during the war.[3]

North Carolina troops had seen a degree of combat even before Caswell took office as governor. There had, of course, been the clash at Moore's Creek Bridge, in which Caswell had been a leading participant. Subsequently, having failed to gain a foothold in North Carolina, the British expedition embarked from Cape Fear on May 31, 1776, to capture—without the help of the North Carolina Loyalists—Charleston, South Carolina. But an American force under the leadership of General Charles Lee, commander of the Southern Department of the Continental Line, defeated the British and denied them a southern foothold in Charleston. The redcoats, led by General Henry Clinton, then sailed in July 1776 to New York, which had become the main headquarters of the British after they evacuated Boston in March. During the fighting at Charleston, 1,400 North Carolina troops served under Brigadier General Robert Howe. When General Washington subsequently summoned Lee to his force in the North, Howe took command of the Southern Department of the Continental Line. Promoted to major general, Howe became the highest-ranking North Carolinian to command Continental troops in the war.[4]

As the conflict continued, North Carolinians served with General Washington's army in the northern theater. In the spring of 1777, North Carolina troops under General Francis Nash joined Washington's main force to defend Philadelphia from the British army marching from New York. They fought at the Battle of Brandywine Creek in September and at Germantown, Pennsylvania, the following month. Those battles ended in defeat for the Americans, and the British occupied Philadelphia. Nash died of wounds sustained at Germantown. Then commanded by General Lachlan McIntosh of Georgia, North Carolina's soldiers suffered through the horrible conditions at Valley Forge in the winter of 1777–78. But in June, the British abandoned Philadelphia and were en route back to New York when Washington's army, including the men from North Carolina, struck them at the Battle of Monmouth Court House in New Jersey. Virtually a stalemate, that clash was the last significant battle fought in the North. Afterward, the major fighting of the war took place in the South.[5]

Throughout the northern campaigns, the problem of finding sufficient funds to support the war effort constantly plagued Caswell, who complained about the weakness of the governorship under the state constitution. An empty state treasury made it difficult to raise, supply and maintain an army. Paper money and bills of credit issued by the state depreciated quickly, and taxes on property and certain commodities never proved sufficient. Many citizens and lawmakers objected to taxation to support a large army. A lack of money to pay and equip soldiers hurt recruiting and led to desertion. Caswell was frustrated in his attempts to obtain financial help from the Continental Congress to support North Carolina's troops.[6] He wrote to Congressman Thomas Burke in Philadelphia in June 1777 begging him, "For God's sake let money be sent out from the continental treasury with the greatest dispatch. The officers here can do nothing in recruiting without money."[7] Several officers threatened to resign if Congress and the General Assembly did not provide more relief in supplies and pay for them and their troops serving outside the state.

The governor continued to press Burke about the urgent need for funds from Congress to arm and equip North Carolina soldiers, but he had little success.[8] Burke and the other North Carolina delegates asked Congress for money and obtained some limited support. But they held out little hope of helping Caswell substantially because "the Continental currency is so much depreciated, that every one sees the necessity of putting an entire stop to emissions, and relying on the Exertions of the States for supplying the public necessities." Furthermore, they noted with perhaps some exaggeration, "The power of the States, internally, is much better understood, much better Established, and . . . much more relied on, than that of Congress."[9] At the same time, the delegates kept Caswell abreast of the activities of Congress and its conduct of the war. They encouraged him to recruit and maintain North Carolina troops in the field and informed him of the discussion and quarrels among the members regarding foreign relations and other policy matters.[10]

Caswell increasingly found the burden of equipping and paying the state's troops resting on his shoulders. Despite his requests, the state legislators remained reluctant to raise taxes, even if they could be paid, and to appropriate revenue for supplies and equipment. The governor was even reduced to begging South Carolina for arms for North Carolina soldiers. Governor Rawlins Lowndes, however, responded that his state did not have enough weapons for its own troops and could not send any to North Carolina.[11]

Caswell especially deplored the wretched circumstances of the troops at Valley Forge. The North Carolina regiments were depleted. Many of the men were starving, underclothed, barefoot and ill. But because of his limited power as governor, he had to rely on the assembly in session to authorize money to relieve their suffering.[12] "Were I to exert every nerve and influence in my power (and no man is more willing than myself), it would be to very little purpose until the Assembly meets," he lamented. Nevertheless, exerting his best efforts and even using his own credit to borrow money, he "was daily buying clothes, leather, skins, salt, pork and provisions, setting manufacturers to work and procuring wagons and boats to send goods on to Pennsylvania."[13]

Lacking in executive powers, Caswell struggled, with limited success, to prevent merchants and others from engaging in profitable wartime speculation with essential supplies. On February 8, 1778, he wrote to the justices of Craven County that he was struggling to obtain clothing, blankets and other "Sundry Goods" desperately needed by North Carolina troops serving with General Washington. "I was," he said, "happy in purchasing a considerable quantity of Cloathing from some French Gentlemen in New Bern, but all I could procure from them is short of what is immediately necessary for our troops at Head quarters." But he had learned that other merchants in New Bern had stockpiles of needed supplies and were hoarding them for maximum profits. And because "it will not be in my power to take the advice of the Council until the last Monday in February instant when that Board is to meet I submit it to you Gentlemen whether under our present unhappy Circumstances you will not think yourselves Justifiable in Ordering those articles . . . to be Seized for public use." He had reports that one particular New Bern merchant was "making other purchases." "[I]f this is true," he declared, "I fear he is one of those Leeches who are Sucking our Blood to enrich themselves. . . . I hope you will think with me that it is Absolutely necessary to give them some Check, especially in those particular Articles we so much want."[14] Nevertheless, despite little support or funding from the General Assembly, Caswell continued to do his best to equip and supply North Carolina's soldiers.

When General Washington reported to him about the lack of clothing and blankets for the North Carolina troops at Valley Forge, Caswell responded:

> *The distresses of the Soldiery for want of Clothing are truly Alarming and the feelings of every Man of the least Sensibility must be wounded on receiving the information of their unhappy circumstances—since I was favoured with your Excellency's account of their sufferings I have been happy in purchasing for our Troops about 4000 Yards of Woolen Cloth, 300 Blankets, 1500 Yards of Ozenbrigs* [osnaburg], *some Shoes and Stockings.*

He had also "purchased a Considerable quantity of Tanned Leather and Deerskins all of which will be sent on to the Clothier General so soon as I can procure waggons."[15]

Washington answered that he was

> *pleased to hear that you have found an opportunity of purchasing a quantity of Cloathing for the Troops of your State, which I beg may be forwarded as quick as possible, not to the Cloathier General but to Brig. Gen.* [Lachlan Mc]*Intosh who commands the North Carolina Troops. My reason for desiring this is, that the Troops of your State will by these means be sure of having the whole appropriated to their particular use, but if it goes into the hands of the Clothier General it will get mixt with the general mass of continental Cloathing, and may be delivered out to the Troops of other States.*

Washington urged Caswell not to have the clothing made from the cloth in North Carolina but to ship the cloth itself to Pennsylvania. "If it comes on in piece as far as Lancaster," declared the general, "it may be made up there in such garments as are most wanted." Washington also encouraged the governor to make every effort to enlist more soldiers "for the completion of Battalions from your State" and send them on to Pennsylvania "as fast as they are raised."[16]

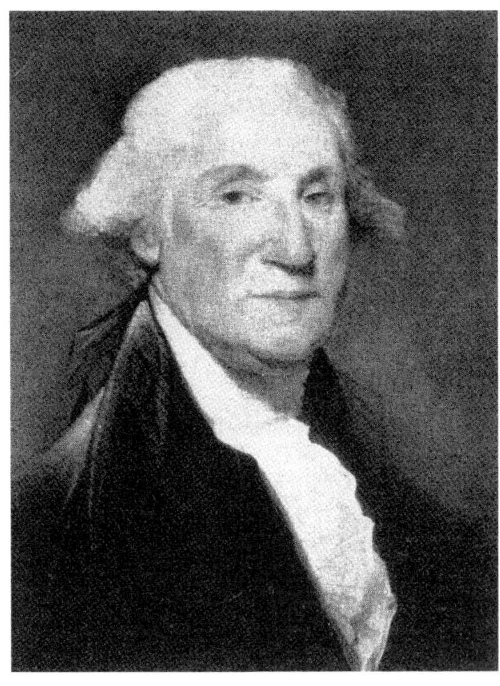

General George Washington relied on Caswell to furnish troops and supplies for the American army.

Caswell replied that he had already sent some of the goods to the clothier general at Lancaster but that in the future they would be "directed to the officer commanding our Brigade." In response to the general's plea for more troops from North Carolina, he informed Washington that "the General Assembly of this state which rose a few days ago passed an Act for the Completion of the Battalions of this state. . . . And I beg leave to assure your Excellency that every means in my power shall be used for raising and forwarding the Men agreeable to your orders."[17]

The continuing failure of the General Assembly to appropriate funds left North Carolina soldiers without adequate equipment and supplies. Rumors circulated throughout the army "that North Carolina did less to supply its officers and men than any other state." Even so, "Washington felt that sending them on, even if not properly fitted out, would give the new recruits less time to desert." However, according to historian Hugh F. Rankin, "The shortages were not because of a lack of effort on the part of Governor Caswell to supply the state's Continental troops."[18] The governor's frustration continued to build as the assembly repeatedly turned down his appeals for funds. At a special session in August 1778, for example, the legislature rejected his earnest plea for money to supply North Carolina's soldiers and suggested that he apply to the Continental Congress. The members of that body, however, remained reluctant to appropriate funds for North Carolina, arguing that the state was not keeping good records of the money already appropriated and even that it was demanding more than the other states. Caswell frequently expressed his frustration at the limited authority the North Carolina Constitution gave him to act as the state's chief executive to deal with the demands of war. "I think if there is any blame to be fixed on those who formed the Constitution," he complained, it was "for cramping so much the powers of the executive."[19]

Caswell attempted to keep in operation the few industries that manufactured war materiel in the state, although his efforts produced little result. But through his exertions, with the cooperation of the assembly, the iron mines and works in Chatham County did produce some iron. Leather manufactories managed to provide a significant number of leather goods, which Caswell ordered shipped to the army in Pennsylvania. The assembly authorized him to purchase all the tin in the state for making canisters. Like the military, the civilian population endured shortages of certain necessities, including food. Salt, important for preserving meat, proved in short supply. From Pennsylvania, John Penn informed Caswell about speculators who were buying up salt in Maryland in order to extort a profit at exorbitant prices, and he alerted the governor to be on the lookout for the same speculators, who were suspected of next going after salt supplies in North Carolina. To help alleviate internal shortages, Caswell issued proclamations against exporting salt, pork and other provisions.[20] From Valley Forge, Washington thanked Caswell for his efforts in supplying his army with salt, "very little of which, to what ought to have been, has been put up to the Northward, owing to the neglect or mismanagement in the Commissary department." Furthermore, the general urged, "I beg you will not discontinue your purchases of Salt

Meat, if it is in your power to extend them, for I am certain we shall have occasion for it."[21]

In addition to the challenges of keeping North Carolina's soldiers and civilians supplied and fed, Caswell had to deal with the attack of the Cherokee Indians on the state's western frontier. Allying themselves with the British, the Cherokee launched an assault on white settlements in the spring of 1776. In response, North Carolina, Virginia, South Carolina and Georgia combined forces to defeat the Indians. General Griffith Rutherford of Salisbury led the North Carolina militia in the campaign. His men destroyed numerous towns of the Indians, ruined their crops, and killed and scalped many of them. Overwhelmed, the Cherokee signed a peace treaty in 1777, giving up claims to all lands east of the Blue Ridge Mountains.

Despite the treaty, problems between the Indians and whites who persisted in encroaching on their lands continued to plague Caswell, who attempted to enforce the terms of the agreement. The British kept up their efforts to stir up the Indians, and the land-greedy settlers' constant violations of the treaty boundaries antagonized the Cherokee. Caswell maintained that the Indians had grounds for anger. He felt that the establishment of a land office in the west was a mistake because it led settlers to believe they could claim land beyond the Blue Ridge. In the face of such violations, Caswell attempted to placate and smooth over relations with the Cherokee to avoid further violence. He informed Savanuca, the Raven of Chota, that he had issued a proclamation announcing punishment for settlers who trespassed on Indian land. He also informed both the Indians and white North Carolinians that the assembly had invalidated all entries of restricted Cherokee land and ordered the return of money rendered by buyers. Afterward, and for the rest of Caswell's tenure as war governor, the relationship between North Carolinians and the Cherokee remained largely peaceful, even though further white encroachment engendered smoldering anger and raids among the Indians.[22]

Caswell also had to defend North Carolina from attacks by the British on the coast. In September 1777, a British expedition landed on Core Banks, where it seized the inhabitants' sheep and cattle. Folks in the vicinity expressed to the governor their concerns about the raid and the possibility that the British might close Ocracoke Inlet to trade. In response, Caswell dispatched militia and some small vessels to drive off the enemy. When the assembly met in November, he called for appropriations for coastal defenses. The assembly, however, deferred a response until its next meeting. When the lawmakers reconvened in 1778, Caswell again informed them that "our coast is much infested with the enemy constantly landing men and plundering."[23]

In early 1778, a fortification called Fort Hancock appeared for coastal defense at Cape Lookout on the southernmost tip of Core Banks. The man most responsible for establishing the fort was a recently arrived French officer: Louis Antoine Jean Baptiste, Chevalier de Cambray-Digny. He was one of a number of ambitious French officers who came to the United States during the Revolution in the hope of gaining military experience and reputation and a position in the American army. He apparently began his American career by offering to assist North Carolina in preparing the state's coastal defenses. In appreciation, the house of commons passed a resolution on April 30 stating "that the House highly approved of Mons. *De Cambray's* Conduct since his arrival in *North Carolina*, that they entertain a most grateful Sense of his disinterested and important services rendered to the State by planning and erecting *Fort Hancock*, and a high Opinion of his Knowledge and abilities in Gunnery and Fortifications." The house requested that Caswell send a copy of the resolution to General Washington and encourage him to appoint Cambray to a position in the Continental Line. The governor complied with the lawmakers' request and wrote to Washington on May 6, 1778:

> *In Pursuance of a Resolution of the General Assembly, of which the enclosed is a copy, I take the liberty of recommending to your Excellency's notice the Bearer Monsieur de Cambray—who arrived in this state about two months ago, since which he has been busily employed here in constructing a Fort at Cape Lookout-Bay, which may be of very great Utility to the states. He wishes you to be informed that his stay here was merely for the service of the States, having refused any allowance from this state for his essential labours. He is desirous of entering into the Army, and I believe has Letters to Congress, and to your Excellency, which make it the less necessary that I should say anything further in respect to him.*[24]

Caswell also dispatched a letter to Congress recommending Cambray for an appointment in the American army. The Frenchman received a commission as lieutenant colonel in the corps of engineers and served in the Monmouth, New Jersey, campaign. In October 1778, Congress ordered him to help with fortifications at Pittsburgh and then to join the American forces in the South. He participated in the defenses of Savannah in 1778 and Charleston in 1780. He was captured on May 12, 1780, and remained a prisoner until exchanged in November 1782. Following a year's leave in France, he received an American discharge as full colonel in November 1783.[25]

Other French officers who attempted to form regiments in North Carolina in 1778 included a Monsieur Chariol and Monsieur Sureau Duvivier, from Guadalupe, who petitioned the General Assembly for authorization to organize French units for the Continental army. The legislature originally granted permission to Chariol but then revoked authorization, "as a sufficient number of privates of the French Nation can not be obtained to compleat the said regiment within this State or the vicinity thereof." The state lawmakers denied Duvivier permission to create a foreign regiment, apparently because such a venture by Chariol was already underway. Duvivier, however, would have been given a commission as a major in Chariol's regiment had it ever been established. After the attempt to form a French regiment failed, Caswell wrote to General Washington recommending Duvivier for a commission in the Continental army. But in April 1779, the Continental Congress had rejected Duvivier's petition and stated that he was "to be Continued in his post of Major in the Continental Service." Caswell also recommended Captain James Montflorence and other officers of the failed regiment to Washington, but evidently their petitions, too, were denied.[26]

Despite Cambray's contribution to North Carolina's coastal defenses, another year passed before legislators acknowledged that the protection of Ocracoke Inlet was "essential and necessary." Even then it remained for the Virginia Assembly finally to purchase a ship, named for Caswell, to defend Ocracoke. When the ship sailed, its captain also had the mission of stopping and searching any vessels that might be violating the governor's proclamations against exporting certain provisions. The ship soon ran aground in Bogue Sound, and Caswell blamed the disaster on the "rascally behavior of the pilots," who apparently resigned when they were not paid.[27]

The governor then called for the assembly to furnish other vessels to defend the coast. The *King Tammany* and the *George Washington* ventured forth but were soon abandoned by the crews when they did not receive their pay. In the end, efforts by state-supported vessels to protect the coast proved unsuccessful. Limited naval success in North Carolina waters was achieved by a number of privateers authorized by Caswell to raid British shipping. Requests by the residents of New Bern and Wilmington for appropriations to establish and maintain local defenses went unheeded by the assembly, and those coastal towns fell easily to the British in 1781.[28]

Caswell and the new state government had considerable trouble with the Loyalists, or Tories, who lived throughout North Carolina. Those North Carolinians who remained loyal to Britain during the Revolution engaged in a number of plots to undermine the state's war efforts, and they conducted raids against powder magazines and other facilities, as well as assisting British troops invading North Carolina. The General Assembly responded with a law requiring Loyalists to take an oath of allegiance or leave the state. The legislature also passed the Confiscation Acts, which authorized the state to seize Loyalists' property and sell it to support the Revolution. Caswell devoted much of his time and energy to attempting to control the Tories, including keeping militiamen in the state who might have served elsewhere. Early in the war, he ordered 150 militiamen to Surry, Rowan and Tryon Counties to suppress Tory uprisings. In other counties, he instructed the militia to protect powder magazines and squelch Loyalist conspiracies. On one occasion, he commanded General Jethro Sumner to imprison a group of Loyalists who had armed themselves in preparation for aiding British regulars.

The so-called Tory War continued well after Caswell ended his third term as governor in April 1780. At the Battle of Ramsour's Mill in Lincoln County in June, the militia defeated a sizable Loyalist force, thereby hindering an invasion of North Carolina by the British, commanded by Cornwallis, who had hoped for Tory support. A large number of Tories also went down in defeat with British troops commanded by Cornwallis's lieutenant, Colonel Patrick Ferguson, at the Battle of Kings Mountain in western North Carolina in October. The most notorious leader of the Loyalists was Colonel David Fanning, whose men rampaged in the state, actually capturing Governor Thomas Burke in a raid on Hillsborough in September 1781.[29]

Not the least of Caswell's constant challenges were recruiting and keeping North Carolina troops in the ranks. The Continental Congress called on North Carolina to provide several regiments or battalions for the national army. As Caswell struggled to fill this request, Congress did not make his task any easier. Acting under the weak Articles of Confederation, Congress never seemed able to appropriate enough money to pay the soldiers and keep them adequately equipped and supplied. It also failed to establish a centralized office for recruiting. Furthermore, as the war continued, enthusiasm for fighting the British in the cause of independence faded, and enlistments dropped. Some officers in the Continental Line were reluctant to obey orders issued by the governor.[30]

From Valley Forge, General Washington complained to Caswell about how few men were serving in North Carolina regiments. "I am really much concerned to find those Regiments so exceedingly short of their Complement of Men," responded Caswell, "and beg leave to Assure you Sir, that every

Attention shall be paid and such Measures adopted as may be in my power to make them more respectable and as nearly complete as possible."[31]

As Washington's army suffered defeats in the North, many of North Carolina's officers in the Continental Line resigned their commissions and left the army. Alarmed by the number of resignations, the General Assembly passed a resolution to curb the number of the state's officers fleeing service. It declared that any North Carolina officer who resigned his commission "at this critical period shall be held and deemed incapable of holding hereafter any office Civil or Military in the gift of the State." The lawmakers instructed Caswell to forward the declaration "to his Excellency General Washington, and that it be published in the news papers of this and the Neighboring States." On November 25, 1777, Caswell dispatched the message to Washington.[32]

One month later, Washington responded to Caswell about the problem of North Carolina officers leaving his army. "A spirit of resigning their commissions from necessary causes or feigned ones I cannot determine," he wrote, "but [it] has been too prevalent in the Army of late. I have discountenanced it as much as possible. . . . The practice is of pernicious tendency and must have an unhappy influence on the service." He told Caswell that he would send the General Assembly's resolution on to the commander of North Carolina troops, "that it may be communicated through their Line."[33]

To compound his difficulties in keeping troops in service, Caswell had only limited authority to order North Carolina soldiers beyond the borders of the state—although the General Assembly did give him authority to call out the militia whenever he deemed it necessary and to send as many as two thousand troops out of state to aid Virginia or South Carolina. The governor also had trouble keeping the state militia up to strength. Riots against service in both the Continental Line and the militia broke out in some counties. Men and officers often proved to be reluctant warriors in units that were poorly trained and equipped and slow in marching. As part-time soldiers subject only to state authority, militia troops were frequently unreliable compared to Continental regulars. Then, too, the militia might have to deal with trouble with Indians and Loyalists, as well as to repel any attack by British regulars.[34]

By the fall of 1778, fears that the British would once again invade the South had reached North Carolina. Indeed, General Henry Clinton intended to carry out his orders to take a defensive position in the North and dispatch an expedition to secure a foothold in a southern port and from there launch a major campaign in the South. At first, it was not certain to the members of the Continental Congress or to North Carolinians where the British might strike—possibly in North Carolina or in a renewed attempt to capture Charleston. Fearful for their home state, congressional delegates from South Carolina—perhaps thinking of Caswell's role at Moore's Creek Bridge in 1776—suggested placing him in command of North Carolina troops in the field with the rank of major general. Caswell considered the proposal but in the meantime remained in office. In October, Congress called on North Carolina to send three thousand troops to South Carolina in anticipation of an attack on Charleston.

Acting on reports that a British force had left New York bound for either the southern states or the West Indies, Caswell issued a proclamation calling furloughed soldiers back to duty, and he commanded the militia to be ready to march southward by November 10. It soon appeared that the British did not intend to land on the coast of South Carolina. Nevertheless, the Continental Congress insisted that North Carolina send troops to bolster the command of General Benjamin Lincoln, operating against a redcoat stronghold in East Florida. North Carolinians resisted such an expedition, but Caswell remained determined to dispatch a force as far south as Charleston. In September, Lincoln had succeeded Howe in command of the Southern Department. A conference with Lincoln at Kingston on November 19 further confirmed Caswell in his decision to prepare for battle below North Carolina's southern border. Also after meeting with Lincoln, he announced that he would not accept command of North Carolina's troops in the southern theater and would remain at the helm in the governor's office.

Instead, Brigadier General John Ashe, a former legislator from New Hanover County, took command of North Carolina's soldiers in the South. Caswell instructed him not to allow the state's militia to be absorbed into the Continental troops of any other state. In late 1778, only about nine hundred North Carolina soldiers had joined Lincoln's force in South Carolina. Early in the following year, they would be marching, along with the rest of Lincoln's men, to Georgia to confront the British expedition that had landed at the port of Savannah. As Lincoln's men drew within twenty-eight miles of the city, they learned that they were too late to help prevent its capture.[35]

On December 23, a British fleet arrived in the harbor at Savannah. Aboard the vessels were 3,500 "redcoats, Hessians, and New York Tories" commanded by Lieutenant Colonel Archibald Campbell. The British plan

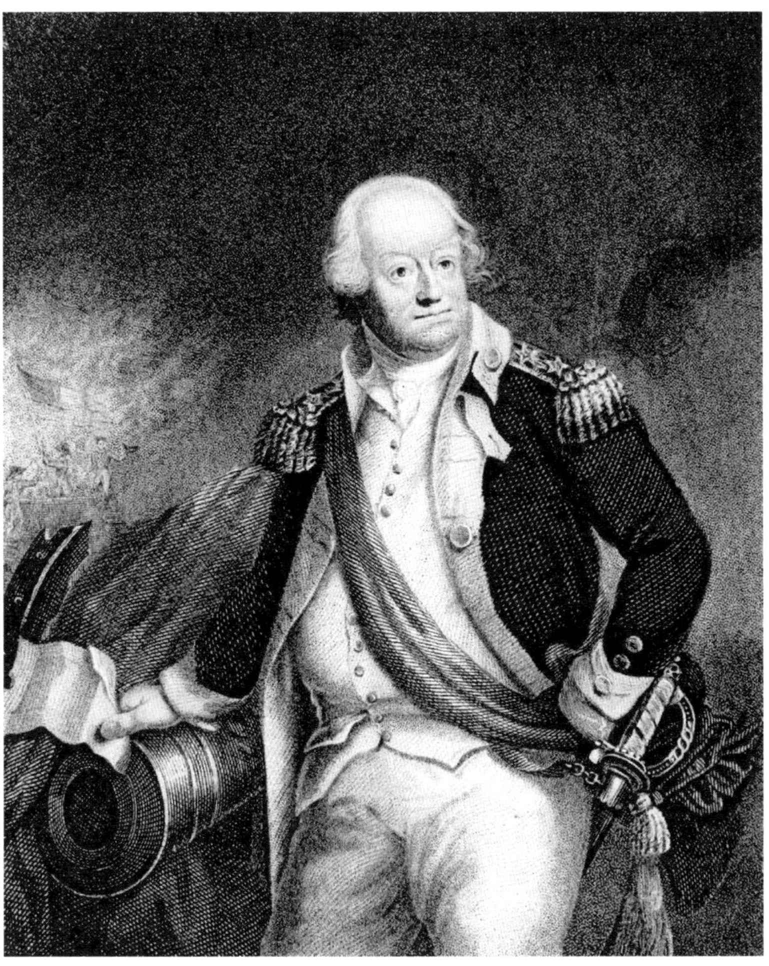

General Benjamin Lincoln.

called for his forces to join with General Augustine Prevost, marching overland from East Florida. Not sure when Prevost might arrive, Campbell decided to attack Savannah with the troops at hand on December 29. He won an easy victory over the Continental Line soldiers and militia under General Howe, who still commanded in Georgia. When Campbell was joined by Prevost, who assumed overall command, their combined force pushed on into Georgia, capturing Augusta in early January 1779. The invasion of South Carolina now loomed as the next British maneuver, and Governor John Rutledge appealed to Caswell for more troops from North Carolina to thwart the invasion.[36]

Alarmed at the threat posed to North Carolina if its neighbor to the south succumbed to British invasion, Caswell increased his efforts to raise troops for service in South Carolina, but with limited success. He again canceled furloughs for Continentals and called up more militia, a sizable number of whom proved reluctant to muster. Although poorly armed and hindered on the march by persistent rains that swelled rivers and creeks, about February 1, 438 of North Carolina's Continentals and a large contingent of militia reached Lincoln's troops "at Purysburg on the South Carolina side of the Savannah River."[37]

From there, Lincoln launched a campaign to reclaim Georgia, but he was daunted when one of his columns, led by General Ashe, was virtually annihilated at Briar Creek on March 3, 1779. Despite that defeat, Lincoln renewed an advance toward Augusta with the ultimate hope of recapturing Savannah. To draw him away, Prevost threatened Charleston in May, which forced Lincoln to rush back there to defend the city. Prevost then withdrew along the coast toward Savannah. In pursuit, the Americans suffered another defeat in a British rearguard action at Stono Ferry, South Carolina, on June 20, 1779. Still in possession of Savannah, the British maintained their foothold in the South. A subsequent joint operation by the Americans and their French allies to take the Georgia port in October 1779 failed decidedly.[38]

During the struggle in South Carolina and Georgia, Caswell maintained a relentless effort to provide troops to Lincoln. His task proved difficult, thankless and sometimes dangerous. At one point, he rushed to Charlotte to spur on militia in the southern counties to Lincoln's side and then hurried to New Bern to urge the assembly to provide further support for the army. His efforts continued to be stymied by legislators reluctant to allocate more funds. Men throughout the state increasingly refused to take up arms in the Continental Line or the militia. Some even threatened to kill Caswell for attempting to draft them into service. One report reached him that a man named Moses Bass, jailed at Kingston for refusing to serve, "watched several days for an opportunity to get a loaded gun and said if he could get one he would be damned to hell if he did not waylay the Road from your house to Kingston and kill you as you passed, for you passed every day that way."[39]

Despite the loss of Savannah, the Americans still held Charleston—but not for long. With the Georgia port securely in British hands, General Henry Clinton moved to win Charleston as his next objective. Assigning command of his headquarters in New York to German general Baron Wilhelm von Knyphausen, Clinton, in late December 1779, embarked for the southern

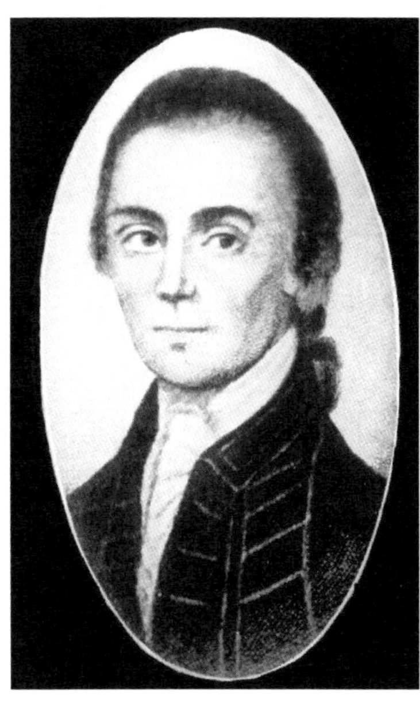
Governor Abner Nash.

theater with 8,700 soldiers and 5,000 sailors and marines aboard a squadron of ships. Having suffered losses in storms en route, the expedition first landed at Savannah for repairs, reorganization and resupply.

The British armada then sailed to the area surrounding Charleston Harbor, appearing there around February 10, 1780. In the port city, General Lincoln garrisoned about 3,600 American troops, with reinforcements on the way, including more militia from North Carolina. Besieged in an ever-tightening encirclement and under relentless bombardment from British naval and land forces, Lincoln surrendered Charleston on May 12. Among the 5,000 American soldiers who laid down their arms were 815 Continentals and 600 militia from North Carolina.[40]

With Charleston securely in British hands, Clinton sailed back to his headquarters at New York, where he faced Washington's army. He assigned his subordinate General Cornwallis to carry on the campaign in the South, which included undertaking offensive operations as long as they did not jeopardize the main mission of holding South Carolina and Georgia. Cornwallis soon determined that the best course of action for holding the South was to invade North Carolina, which still could muster resistance, and then move into Virginia, where Clinton might send him reinforcements.[41]

By the time of the surrender at Charleston, however, an exhausted Richard Caswell had ended his third regular term as governor. For some years, he had suffered from ill health, which included severe headaches, dizziness and other symptoms, probably caused by hypertension. The term expired in April, and his successor, Abner Nash, soon took up the office of North Carolina's chief executive.[42]

Chapter 5

Battlefield Command in the Carolinas

Despite his growing health problems, there was no respite for Caswell when his term as governor ended. He immediately traded one leadership role for another in the cause of American independence. Upon leaving the office of governor, he was appointed by the General Assembly as a major general and commander of the North Carolina militia. The legislators wanted him to raise four thousand militiamen and march into South Carolina with as much haste as he could muster. Caswell's new position annoyed Nash, who felt that the appointment was unconstitutional and that Caswell's authority to appoint staff officers infringed on Nash's powers as governor.[1]

Meanwhile, before beginning his invasion of North Carolina, Cornwallis attempted to build a base of operations at Camden, South Carolina. At that site, he would soon clash with the forces of General Horatio Gates, who replaced Lincoln in July as commander of the Southern Department. Gates was known as the hero of the northern Battle of Saratoga, in which the Americans had achieved a major victory over a British force commanded by General John Burgoyne in the autumn of 1777. Upon reaching North Carolina, the egotistical Gates immediately began an ill-prepared and poorly planned march on Camden, which Cornwallis strongly reinforced in anticipation of an American attack.[2]

Caswell did his best to gather the often-reluctant North Carolina militiamen and set them on the road toward Camden. In June, he began forming his troops at Cross Creek, where he reported to Governor Nash that the

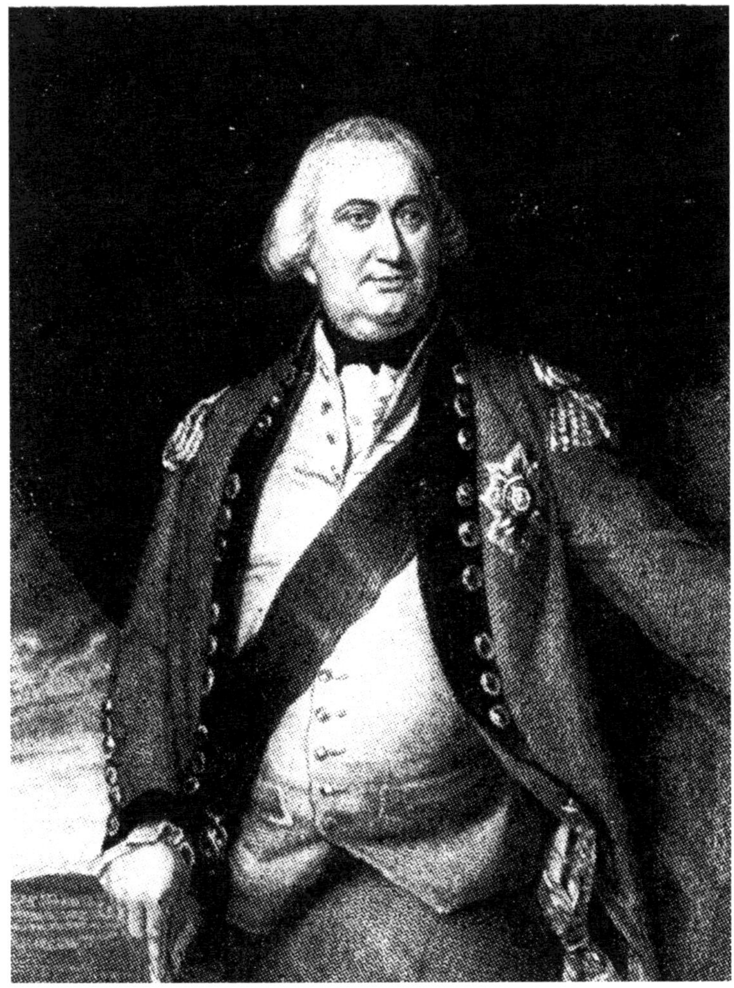

British general Lord Charles Cornwallis.

enlistment of militia proved disappointing and problematic in both numbers and quickness of response. He also noted the lack of sufficient arms and equipment and encouraged Nash to press the General Assembly for funds to purchase much-needed weapons and supplies. In July, he moved his men to Coxe's Mill, where the Continentals were mustering. In the meantime, Gates was en route to that site from Hillsborough. But Caswell left before the commanding general arrived, moving his militia into the Yadkin River Valley, where he anticipated procuring more crops to feed his soldiers. That movement, however, left him open to accusations that he removed from the camp at Coxe's Mill because he resented the authority of the Continental officers and perhaps wanted to earn exclusive fame in any coming action.[3]

Certainly Caswell and Gates did not work particularly well together. Gates accused Caswell of making efforts intended only to bolster his own military reputation. He further charged that Caswell was slow in having his militia join Gates's overall command and that he allowed the North Carolinians to consume an inequitable share of supplies. As he moved toward Anderson, South Carolina, Gates complained to Caswell that

> *I suffer very* [*sic*] *Distress for want of provisions, and know not, if I can expect, where I am going, any Relief from you. General* [Griffith] *Rutherford's and your Commands, have gleaned the Country on both Sides of the River, and the Virginia Militia stick in my Rear, and devour all that comes forward; This is a Mode of conducting War, I am a Stranger to. The Whole should support and sustain the Whole, or the parts will soon go to Decay.*[4]

He wanted to give Caswell "a rap over the knuckles." But he realized that he needed the North Carolina militia and that if he disciplined Caswell, "the militia would disperse."[5] Gates, however, was known for an "offensive personality" that often made his relationships with other officers difficult.[6] His own abrasiveness and attitude of self-importance after his significant victory at Saratoga might have led to his condescending criticism of Caswell.

Nevertheless, the two commanders managed to cooperate in the campaign against Cornwallis. As he made plans, Gates sought the opinions of Caswell and General Griffith Rutherford, who commanded a brigade of North Carolina militia. Caswell responded that reports on British movements varied and remained inconclusive, but he believed that the redcoats were consolidating at Camden, where they might stand and fight. Gates disregarded this intelligence initially, preferring to believe that Cornwallis had moved to Savannah, thereby weakening his force at Camden. Caswell agreed with Gates that they should combine their troops. Caswell informed him that he would consolidate the North Carolina militia units and join Gates's main force near Anderson, South Carolina. By August 7, Caswell had united his 2,100 militia with Gates's "grand army."[7]

The ensuing Battle of Camden on August 16 proved disastrous for the Americans. Gates's ill-conceived plan left his flanks "in the air." He positioned his militia, which included troops from Virginia and South Carolina, on the left of his line facing British regulars and held half of his regulars in reserve. Caswell's troops stood near the center of the line of militia, and his men "were swept from the field" with the first wave of troops retreating in the face of the British assault. With the redcoats' overwhelming strike, the Virginia and then the North Carolina militia broke and ran, throwing away arms and equipment. Many never fired a shot. In Caswell's command, only the militia led by Lieutenant Colonel Henry Dixon, aligned next to the Delaware Continentals, held its position and fought. Cornwallis's troops quickly gained the field, and the Americans' defeat was complete. Estimates

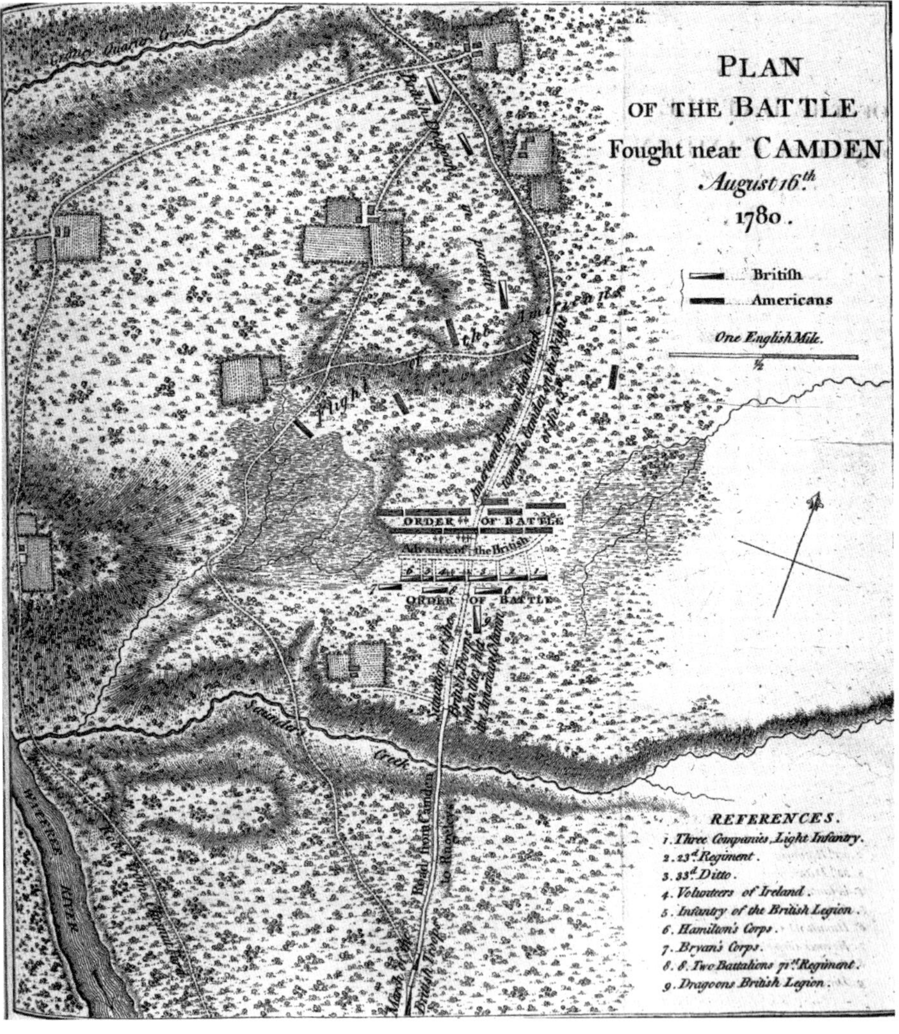

The Battle of Camden.

of casualties vary, but Gates lost probably eight to nine hundred soldiers killed and another thousand taken prisoner. Of Caswell's militia, between sixty-three and one hundred men were killed and perhaps as many as three hundred captured. Most of those casualties were in Dixon's regiment.[8]

The retreat of the American troops became a rout as they fled back into North Carolina. "The torrent of unarmed militia bore away with it Generals Gates, Caswell, and a number of others, who soon saw that all was lost," recalled Maryland officer Colonel Otho Holland Williams.[9] Caswell made three attempts to rally his men and establish an orderly withdrawal, but his efforts failed. He then withdrew to Charlotte, where he made considerable effort to consolidate the scattered militia to oppose further British advancement.

From there on August 19, he wrote to Governor Nash that he assumed the chief executive had already received news of "our unfortunate defeat by the enemy near Camden the 16th Inst." from General Gates, who had started for Hillsborough two days earlier. Meanwhile, "On my arrival at Charlotte I immediately issued orders for the Scattered Troops to repair to that place & for those who were in our rear at the Time of the defeat . . . to March also to Charlotte. I have likewise called on all the Militia in the Counties of Rowan, Mecklenburg & Lincoln to Assemble tomorrow at the same place, they are gathering fast & I make no doubt we shall make a formidable Camp in a few days." He noted that the militia were woefully short of weapons and ammunition because "our people in the panick were so lost to their own Security & Service of their Country as to throw away their Arms & cartridge boxes." He therefore requested that arms and lead shot recently purchased in Virginia be sent to his camp as quickly as possible. Concerned about casualties and the condition of his troops captured by the British, he further reported, "Yesterday I dispatched Dr. [Hugh] Williamson, from Charlotte, with a Flag to the British Camp in order to [obtain] a List of the Killed wounded and Prisoners of our unhappy Countrymen & to Assist the Wounded, if they allow him to stay for the latter purpose, he has two Light Horsemen with him by whom I expect a return in a few days."[10]

Once he had collected a force at Charlotte, Caswell intended to place them under the command of a subordinate and then travel to Hillsborough, where he anticipated the General Assembly was soon to meet, "unless it shall appear that my presence with the Army is absolutely necessary or your orders prevent it," he told Nash. However, "having lost all our public & private Stores, I shall have to take the Field with only my Blanket, without a Tent or any Camp necessaries." Furthermore, Caswell's deteriorating health had led him to conclude that he could not effectively remain in command of the militia. "My Constitution will not Support me long in that Situation & my present weak State of Health with the Fatigues I am daily obliged to undergo will soon render me unfit for any Command," he complained. He was not sure what officer might replace him. "I fear," he informed the governor,

> *Genl. Rutherford is Killed or Captured,* [General John] *Butler &* [General Isaac] *Gregory are missing, Gregory's Horse was killed under him, Rutherford received a wound in his thigh. But I saw Butler in the retreat, since which I have heard nothing from him. I will endeavor to find him out & if he is living & able to take Charge of the Troops give him the Command when I leave them.*

Regarding a pressing meeting of the state lawmakers, Caswell advised Nash:

> *If your Excellency does not find a Sufficient Number of Members to Constitute the General Assembly at Hillsborough I submit to you the propriety of appointing a Meeting of the Body at this place* [Charlotte] *where the greater No. of the members belonging to the Army could attend & where the State of matters Relating to the Army could be with greater certainty and precision understood, if no Assembly meets, Certainly your Excellency & Council will repair here.*[11]

But the General Assembly managed to convene at Hillsborough, and Caswell then left camp for that town, although he did not linger there but traveled on to Chatham County, where he helped organize a brigade of eight hundred militiamen. On September 3, he and his subordinate General Jethro Sumner began leading that force to Salisbury in further preparation for repelling a British invasion from South Carolina.[12]

On September 8, Cornwallis broke camp at Camden and began marching his troops on the road to Charlotte. Accompanying him was former royal governor Josiah Martin, who continued to contend that a large number of Loyalists would rally to the invading British. Cornwallis's plan was to drive into the middle of North Carolina, passing through Charlotte, Salisbury, Salem, Guilford Court House and Hillsborough. At Hillsborough, his army would acquire more recruits and supplies.

As he began his march into North Carolina, Cornwallis dispatched Major James Craig to secure the port of Wilmington as a possible source for

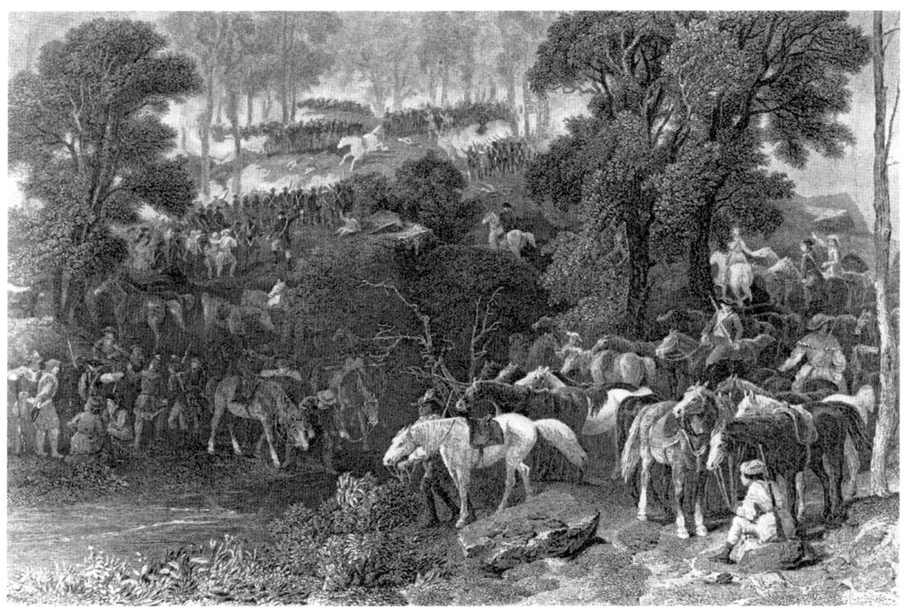

A scene at the Battle of Kings Mountain.

reinforcements and supplies. The general ordered Major Patrick Ferguson, on his left flank, to campaign in western North Carolina, where it was anticipated that a large number of Loyalists would join Ferguson's invasion force.

Cornwallis found, however, that events did not transpire as he had hoped. Craig easily took control at Wilmington. But as the British main column moved toward Charlotte, it was harassed and depleted by hit-and-run tactics from partisans. Then came news that Ferguson had been defeated by Patriot militia and the Over-Mountain Men at the Battle of Kings Mountain on October 7, 1780. Fearful that the Whigs in the western region could now attack his South Carolina outposts, Cornwallis withdrew his main force back into South Carolina to regroup with reinforcements.[13]

While the British campaign was unfolding in North Carolina, Caswell learned that he had been replaced as commander of the state militia. On September 12—one day prior to adjournment—the General Assembly gave command of the state militia to General William Smallwood, a Maryland Continental. Caswell turned over command of the militia brigade near Salisbury to General Sumner. Sumner then marched his force southward to connect with the other militia near Charlotte to oppose any British invasion. But annoyed that he was passed over for command of the state militia after Caswell's removal, Sumner resigned from service, although he later returned to recruiting duty and command of militia in the summer and fall of 1781.[14]

In the meantime, on September 6, 1780, Governor Nash had appealed to the General Assembly to create a North Carolina Board of War to help in the overwhelming task of maintaining the war effort in opposing Cornwallis's invasion of North Carolina after his victory at Camden. The legislature established a five-member board "but went far beyond the governor's request to create an advisory body." In fact,

> *the new agency was given powers that exceeded limitations imposed by the state constitution. Its members were given extraordinary powers in raising, organizing, and equipping the military forces of the state. They were to concert with the commanding officer in the state plan of operations, requiring prompt troop returns and accurate records. Their authority included the right to remove or suspend all military officers of the state and appoint others to their places. The executive was required to carry through with all measures formulated by the board "as necessary and expedient for the public safety."*[15]

During the four and a half months that it operated, the board oversaw military operations for North Carolina in the campaign against the army of Cornwallis. It mobilized troops and supplies and communicated with commanders in the Continental Line in North and South Carolina and with Governor Thomas Jefferson of Virginia. It also corresponded with Governor Nash at the capital in New Bern, informing him of its actions and directing his attention to certain problems.

But resentful of the board's power, which went well beyond what he had intended, Nash cooperated with that body reluctantly and only when he considered it essential. The friction and lack of cooperation between the two entities sometimes led to inefficiency in military preparations and operations. To the General Assembly convened at Halifax in January 1781, the governor vowed to resign if the legislature did not give him power over the board's decisions. In response, the lawmakers replaced the Board of War with a three-member Council Extraordinary to advise the governor on war policy.[16]

After being replaced by Smallwood, Caswell—perhaps temporarily improved in health and regretting his withdrawal from the militia or perhaps piqued that command of North Carolinians had been given to the Marylander—informed Governor Nash at New Bern that he was again prepared "to take the Field & waited his Orders only." Nash responded that the General Assembly had given the Board of War virtual control over the militia and that he was powerless to reinstate Caswell. Angered by that response, Caswell asked the governor if he still regarded him as a general officer. The governor answered that "he did not, that the Resolution appointing General Smallwood to the Command of the Militia of this State [was] a Supersedas to General Caswell's Command as Major General." In that case, declared the seething Caswell, he would also resign his position on the North Carolina Board of Trade. With a degree of sympathy for Caswell, Nash appealed to the Board of War for another command for Caswell. Board chairman Alexander Martin suggested that the board give Caswell a new military assignment.[17]

The board then recommended "a separate command for Major General Caswell," and in February 1781, the General Assembly restored him to command of militia and Continental troops in eastern North Carolina, with the rank of major general. In that same month, he was elected to the state senate and appointed to serve on the new Council Extraordinary, along with Allen Jones and Alexander Martin.[18]

Following Cornwallis's retreat into South Carolina, General Gates moved his army to Charlotte to oppose another possible invasion by the British from that state. But Gates's days as commander were numbered. On December 5, General Nathanael Greene arrived to replace him as the head of the Southern Department of the Continental army. Because of Gates's poor performance at the Battle of Camden, Congress had instructed General Washington to remove him. Pleased with Greene's past performance in his army, Washington chose the "fighting Quaker" from Rhode Island as Gates's replacement.

Determining that the area around Charlotte did not include enough forage to sustain his troops, Greene moved his main force to the banks of the Yadkin–Pee Dee River in South Carolina, where provisions were more plentiful. He ordered another detachment, under the command of General Daniel Morgan, to southwest South Carolina near a British outpost at the town of Ninety Six. Greene anticipated that dividing his force in that manner would allow the two wings to observe British movements closely and scrounge more effectively for food for the American soldiers. Furthermore, if Cornwallis renewed his march northward into North Carolina, he would be moving between the two American commands, which could assault his flanks. For Cornwallis, of course, Greene's dividing his army into two parts gave the British the opportunity to defeat each part separately.

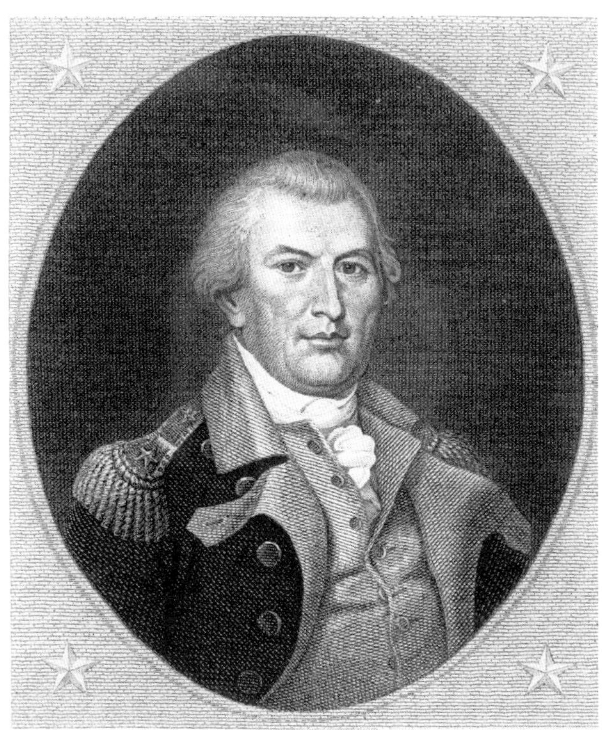

Left: General Nathanael Greene.

Below: The Battle of Cowpens.

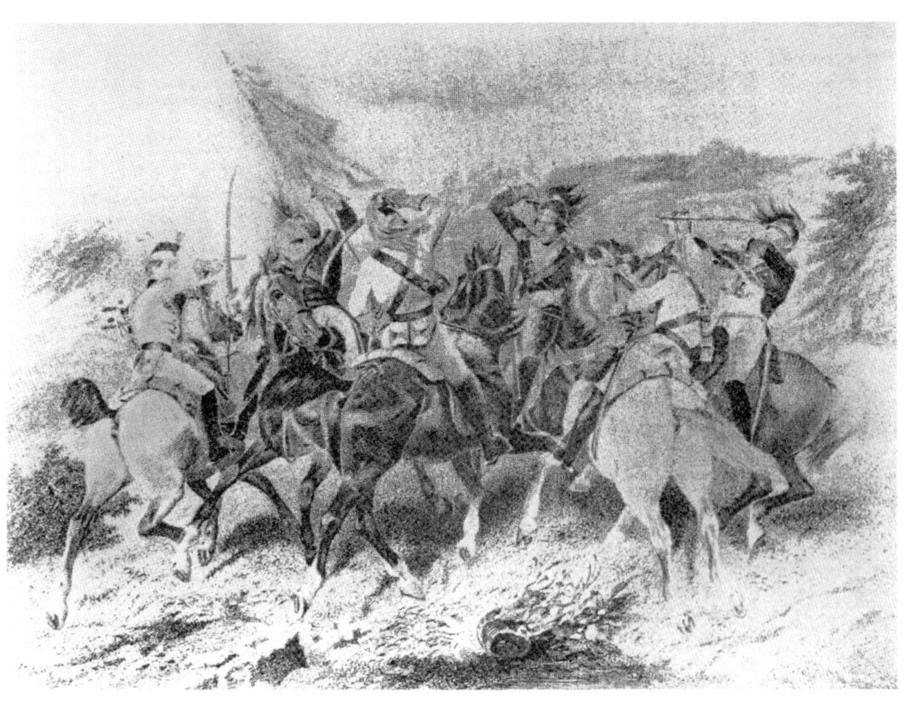

Cornwallis decided to attack the smaller force, led by Morgan, and destroy it first. To accomplish that mission, he sent Lieutenant Colonel Banastre Tarleton and his legion to corner and wipe out Morgan's troops. Morgan retreated before the oncoming British until he took a stand at Hannah's Cowpens on the Broad River in South Carolina. At the ensuing Battle of Cowpens, Tarleton's legion suffered a devastating defeat. The British colonel himself barely escaped with a few men and fled back to Cornwallis's main camp with news of the disaster. Morgan, meanwhile, wasted no time in moving northward into North Carolina because he knew that the main British army would soon try to overtake his troops.[19]

Indeed, enraged over the American victory at Cowpens, Cornwallis began a hot pursuit of Morgan, who withdrew to Charlotte. Meanwhile, Greene left his other column under the leadership of General Isaac Huger—with orders to move northward toward Salisbury and Guilford Court House—while he, Greene, hastened to take command of Morgan's retreating force. Greene then skillfully eluded the three thousand invading British troops, staying ahead of them and drawing them farther and farther into the Piedmont of North Carolina. Finding his progress hindered by swollen rivers and streams, bad weather and difficult terrain, Cornwallis could not catch the retreating Americans. Frustrated with his lack of success, he discarded or burned baggage and equipment in an effort to speed his progress. The Quaker general finally crossed the Dan River into Virginia, and Cornwallis paused at Hillsborough, where he announced that he was there to rescue Loyalists in the area.

Safely out of reach, Greene united his two columns and further reinforced his army with new recruits to a strength of 4,000 soldiers. He had weakened Cornwallis's force by compelling it to endure a hard march in the dead of winter and drawing it more than two hundred miles from its base of supply. Greene anticipated that Cornwallis might pass through Halifax in eastern North Carolina in pursuit of him in Virginia. He therefore had Caswell consolidate troops at Halifax. The town stood strategically on the Roanoke River and along the road from Wilmington to Petersburg, Virginia. It also held a large store of supplies. Greene dispatched his chief engineer, Colonel Thaddeus Kosciuszko, to fortify the town. He requested that Caswell provide men to assist the colonel and occupy Halifax when the fortifications were finished. In addition, Caswell shipped provisions from Halifax to Greene in Virginia, along with a brigade of 1,500 men.[20]

Greene then crossed back into North Carolina with the objective of engaging Cornwallis in battle. The two men's armies clashed at Guilford

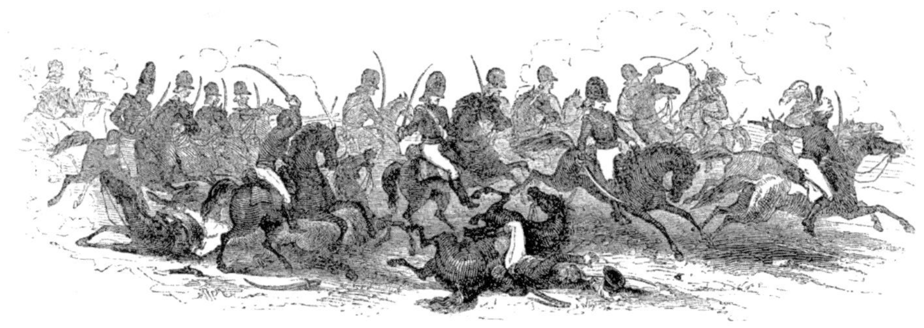

Cavalry charge at the Battle of Guilford Court House.

Court House on March 15, 1781. In the ferocious fighting, the Americans, including the North Carolina militia, inflicted heavy casualties on the British. However, Greene withdrew from the battlefield first, leading Cornwallis to claim victory. That boast prompted British politician and war critic Charles James Fox to proclaim sarcastically that "another such victory would destroy the British army." In any event, Cornwallis was sufficiently weakened that he could not resume the offensive. He therefore began marching his army to Wilmington for rest, reinforcements and supplies. He reached the port city on April 7. Greene meanwhile moved his troops into South Carolina and Georgia to hold key points and thereby thwart support for Cornwallis from the south. Despite a failure to carry the field at the Battle of Eutaw Springs, South Carolina—the last major battle in the South—in September, Greene managed to neutralize the British in South Carolina and Georgia, leaving them with only a weak occupation of the ports of Charleston and Savannah.[21]

At Wilmington, Major Craig, who held and fortified the town, had sent out patrols to raid the Whig population in the surrounding countryside. Craig's men—sometimes aided by Tories—captured a number of Patriot leaders, including Cornelius Harnett and General John Ashe, and confined them to an open blockhouse in Wilmington. Harnett weakened while imprisoned and died on April 28, 1781, shortly after his release. Also while held in Craig's "Bull Pen," Ashe contracted smallpox. When released, he died en route to unite with his family in Hillsborough in October 1781.[22]

Unable to confront and destroy Greene's army, Cornwallis determined to invade Virginia, and he departed Wilmington on April 25, 1781, marching northward through eastern North Carolina. Clinton had not authorized him to move into Virginia, but Cornwallis reasoned that he could unite there with other British troops under the command of Generals Benedict Arnold and William Phillips, who had invaded that state.[23] Along the route, his soldiers and local Tories terrorized the Whig population. "Once again," writes Rankin,

> *the red-coated army was on the move. Trudging along the rutted, sandy roads, they marched slowly and almost deliberately into Duplin County. The entire countryside was terrorized. Tories and other hangers-on, who followed the British army like a flight of vultures, plundered every farm and plantation along the way. Some homes roared up in a mass of flames and smoke-blackened chimneys marked the path of the marching column. Horses and cattle were driven off, and slaves were forced to come along with the army. Many Whigs loaded their families and most valuable possessions into wagons and hastened to a safer area.*[24]

Cornwallis marched his troops through Halifax, but they apparently encountered no resistance at the town from Caswell's militia. Their only clash with the Americans occurred at Peacock's Bridge, south of Halifax. In a skirmish at that site, Tarleton's cavalry drove off five hundred men commanded by Colonel David Gorham. After a brief rest in Halifax, Cornwallis's column moved on into Virginia, arriving at Petersburg on May 20. Cornwallis had left his sick and wounded at Wilmington and had given Craig orders to leave that city when he reached Virginia. Craig, however, maintained that he should do what he could to support the Loyalists and wreak havoc on the American rebels in North Carolina. He raided into Duplin County, where he won a skirmish at Rockfish Creek, and then marched on to New Bern, where his troops encamped for two days.[25]

In the violent inner civil war between Loyalists and Whigs in North Carolina, each faction committed atrocities against the other. Five Loyalists or Tories were executed at Kingston in 1780, reportedly in retaliation for the harsh treatment and imprisonment of Whigs captured by Loyalists and turned over to British officers. Those Patriots thrown in irons aboard a British warship included Samuel and William Ashe, sons of General John Ashe and nephews of Samuel Ashe, a Revolutionary leader, judge, Speaker of the senate and future governor. Traditionally, Richard Caswell has been credited with ordering the execution of the Tories. However, the retaliatory killing appears to have been ordered and carried out not by Richard Caswell but by his son William, commander of the New Bern militia.[26]

In protest of that and other acts of reprisal inflicted by the militia, Major Craig appealed to Governor Nash to take measures to restrain "the inhuman treatment of the King's friends on every occasion and by every part of the militia in arms." He made special mention of William Caswell's orders for the executions, and he pointed out that he was having difficulty restraining enraged Loyalists from retaliating by killing prisoners held by the British. Craig wrote to Nash that if he had "listened only to the first emotions excited by the account of Mr. Caswell's conduct in *murdering* five men at Kingston," he would have executed Samuel and William Ashe in retaliation. But, he declared, "fortunately for them I am a soldier and have been taught to look on the deliberate & unnecessary shedding of blood to be repugnant to my principles." Craig further noted that "several instances which have happened since both in that quarter [Kingston] and in Duplin County have very nearly forced me to have recourse to the expedient I wish to avoid."

He insisted that he was complaining directly to Governor Nash because to appeal to Caswell or other militia officers would be useless. But he vowed that if executions of Loyalists did not stop, he would have no choice but to respond in like fashion by permitting the execution of Whig prisoners. "After allowing a reasonable time for the interposition of your authority," he informed Nash, "I shall think myself called upon by Justice, Duty & I may add ultimately by very consideration of humanity, to give the people who from the most laudable principles of loyalty take arms in the King's favor, ample revenge & satisfaction for every instance of *murder* committed by any party of Militia on one of them, and for this purpose I shall not hesitate to deliver over to them those Prisoners who from character or situation are most likely to gratify them in those sentiments."[27]

On May 28, Governor Nash wrote to William Caswell that Craig had informed him that the British commander holding the Whig prisoners "declares his Instructions to retaliate on them for the unjustifiable Measure said to be adopted by yr. Men and only forbears till the matter represented" can be further verified. The governor was convinced that William Caswell would not have executed the Tories just for capturing Whigs and turning them over to the British regulars for imprisonment. Therefore, Nash continued, "I request you Sir to State the Affair as it ought to be for I cannot think that the measure, so unsoldierly could have been effected by your permission much less Direction." He allowed that instead of merely taking legitimate prisoners of war, the executed Loyalists must have been "villains" and not "under the Directions by the particular command of any British officer." They had to have been a "lawless band, fugitives from justice, common thieves & deserters from the militia." The governor instructed William Caswell "to dispatch" to Craig "a full representation of the affair &

show the real causes" for the execution of the Tories in order to prevent the deaths of the Whig prisoners.[28]

It is not known whether William Caswell explained to Craig his actions in executing the Tories, but he continued his efforts to suppress Loyalists. He issued a proclamation granting them amnesty if they surrendered. Receiving little response to that and subsequent messages, he issued this final notice on May 31, 1781:

> *I am very sorry to find that you have slighted my Proclamation and so little regard different Letters which I have sent you. I do now for the last time in the most earnest manner request you to come in and deliver yourselves up and become good Citizens to the State. I assure you it is not my wish to distress a Single Individual of you, but I am an officer of the State and must do the Duty thereof. You may therefore rely on it that if you do not come and Submit that I will use every Step that I can take to destroy you, this must be done as we may live in peace. Let your own reason Dictate for you in this case and I am Sensible you will not Hesitate one moment in comeing in. Should you not Determine this way your Blood be upon your own heads as you may at this Critical juncture prevent its being Shed.*[29]

Although no evidence has been found that Craig ever endorsed retaliatory or summary executions of Patriot prisoners, some Whigs, such as the aforementioned Harnett and John Ashe, died as a result of their harsh imprisonment in Wilmington. The Tory War continued in North Carolina for a time, even after fighting between the main armies had ceased. David Fanning, who led more than nine hundred Loyalists in a campaign against Whigs, was the most notorious of the militant Tories. He and his band marauded throughout the state, pillaging, burning and killing. After capturing Governor Thomas Burke, his council and a large number of army officers in Hillsborough in September 1781, Fanning marched them to the British prison in Wilmington. Burke was subsequently paroled on James Island in Charleston. However, he broke his parole in January 1782 and returned to North Carolina. In early May 1782, Fanning left North Carolina, and he remained in Charleston until he set out for Nova Scotia in 1784. His departure from North Carolina ended the bitter inner civil war between Tories and Whigs in the state.

Loyalists, too, had been victims, often being attacked by Whigs. The state government also seized and sold their property under the authority of its Confiscation Acts. Some Tories were imprisoned or expelled from North

Carolina, and others fled during and after the war to such places as Nova Scotia and the Bahamas. Those who remained or returned to the state after the war received pardons under North Carolina's Act of Pardon and Oblivion in April 1783. Some who had their property confiscated attempted to recover it, but they had little success.[30]

Not at all pleased that Cornwallis had invaded Virginia in the spring of 1781, General Clinton ordered him to march his force to the Chesapeake area, where he should establish a naval base and prepare to send troops to New York for possible operations along the Delaware River. Clinton further instructed Cornwallis that he might harass the enemy but was not to undertake a full campaign. But Cornwallis had already launched raids against Richmond and Charlottesville, and his troops narrowly missed capturing Governor Thomas Jefferson, who had fled before them.

Cornwallis encamped at Williamsburg, where he received Clinton's orders on June 26, which were followed by a further request to dispatch six of his infantry regiments, supported by cavalry and artillery, to New York. Cornwallis then marched his men to Portsmouth, from where he intended to dispatch troops for New York. But before he arrived there, word came from Clinton requesting that he prepare to send troops to Pennsylvania instead of New York. As he began loading men for Philadelphia, further instructions arrived from Clinton to hold back some for New York. Apparently, Cornwallis then received further orders to fortify the area around Yorktown and deploy any troops he could spare to New York. Ultimately, he decided to retain his entire force and establish fortifications at Yorktown. On August 2, he placed his soldiers at that site, and Clinton did not object to the maneuver. The encampment at Yorktown proved Cornwallis's downfall, for he would be encircled and trapped there by Washington's army and a sizable French army and naval force and compelled to surrender on October 19, 1781.[31] Hearing of the surrender, and threatened by a militia force commanded by General Griffith Rutherford north of Wilmington, Craig evacuated his soldiers and some Loyalists from the town and sailed to Charleston.[32]

Technically, the surrender at Yorktown did not end the Revolutionary War. The British still held vital points, including New York, Charleston and Savannah, as well as Canada and part of the West Indies. With Cornwallis's capitulation, however, Parliament and other government officials, tired of a long and costly war, no longer wanted to continue the struggle to retain Britain's American colonies. The Treaty of Paris would officially conclude the separation and set the new United States on its own course.[33]

In the treaty, signed in Paris in September 1783, Britain acknowledged the independence of the new nation, and boundaries were set between Canada and the United States. Under the terms, both Britain and the United States would have free navigation of the Mississippi River. Americans would be permitted to fish off Newfoundland and Nova Scotia and to cure fish on the unsettled beaches of Labrador, the Magdalen Islands and Nova Scotia. Citizens of each country were obligated to pay their creditors in the other nation, and no one from either would receive punishment for his actions in the war. All hostilities must end, and Britain's troops had to evacuate the United States "with all convenient speed." Congress ratified the treaty in January 1784, and the two sides exchanged ratifications in May.[34]

Chapter 6

Postwar Career, Western Lands and the United States Constitution

By the time of Yorktown, Caswell's military career had ended in North Carolina. Evidently, his last military experience had been his efforts to suppress demonstrations against the draft in Duplin County in June 1781. Then, leaving his son William, a brigadier general of the New Bern District, to deal with the Tories in eastern North Carolina, he entered into new land speculation in western North Carolina. Apparently, his journey to the area beyond the mountains fulfilled a wish that he had held for some time and might have been an attempt to improve his financial circumstances, which had suffered during the war. In the course of his 1781 western trip, Caswell surveyed thousands of acres that he had acquired in Washington, Sullivan and Greene Counties in what is now the state of Tennessee. Land transactions recorded in North Carolina reveal that he purchased 2,640 acres in present-day Tennessee in the vicinity of Big Limestone Creek, Boone's Creek and Walnut Valley and on an island in the French Broad River. In 1782, Caswell joined William Blount, Joseph Martin and John Donelson in forming the Muscle Shoals Land Company to buy a tract on the Tennessee River. The fertile bottomland held considerable promise for speculators and settlers, who sought to buy the land from its Indian occupants, including the Cherokee, Creek and Chickasaw. Griffith Rutherford and John Sevier—a militia commander and popular political leader in the western counties and a friend of Caswell—along with other investors soon signed on with the company and attempted to purchase the land from the Cherokee in the

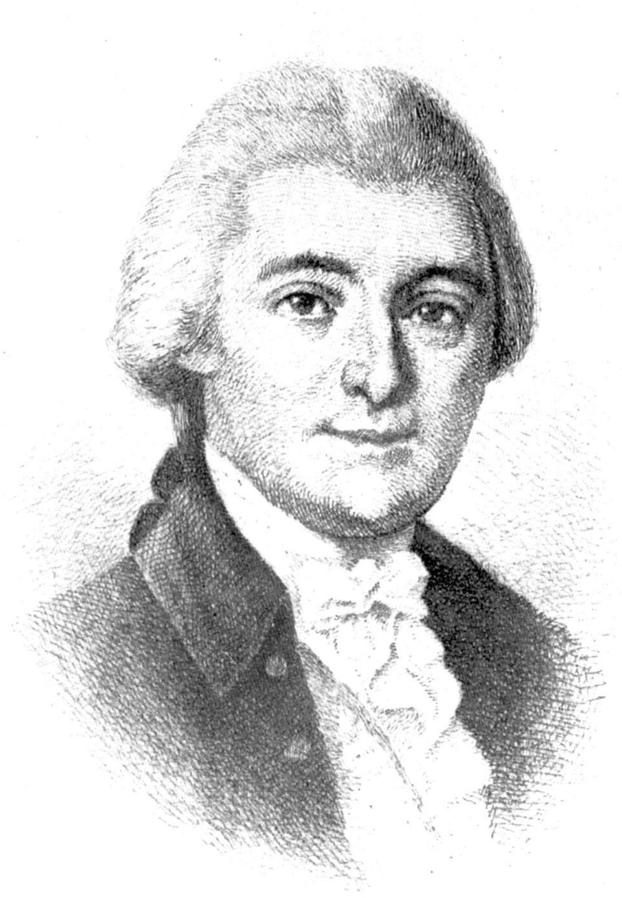

William Blount.

fall of 1783. In that same year, a North Carolina law opened vast tracts in the West for purchase and speculation.

However, Georgia and South Carolina also claimed the area wanted by Caswell and his fellow speculators. Blount attempted to persuade Georgia to create a new county in the region, for which the investors would serve as officials, and Sevier tried to woo the Spanish to the south into supporting the company's scheme for acquisition. In the end, however, all those speculative plans and the company failed, although speculators continued to develop schemes to acquire the fertile Muscle Shoals tract.

Postwar Career, Western Lands and the United States Constitution

In the meantime, Caswell had returned to North Carolina and relinquished his final duties with the militia, and the voters of Dobbs County had elected him to the state senate. Upon assuming his seat in April 1782, he was elected Speaker, a position to which he was reelected in 1783 and 1784. Also, shortly after he arrived in the senate, the General Assembly appointed him to the office of comptroller general, with the assignment of dealing with the state's suffering postwar finances. In that capacity, he labored to resolve the financial difficulties that had developed with the Continental Congress during the Revolution, including ensuring that North Carolina troops who served in the Continental Line received their pay.[1]

Caswell soon found himself embroiled in considerable political controversy involving North Carolina's western lands and the state's relationship with the new national government operating under the Articles of Confederation. In its Cession Act in the spring of 1784, North Carolina ceded its western lands—between the mountains and the Mississippi River—to the federal government as part of the settlement of the state's Revolutionary War debt. The United States Congress had requested cession of states' western territories for land sales to reduce the war debt and ultimately to establish new states. As Caswell followed the legislative debate over the Cession Act, he noted that it "has been much debated particularly in the House of Commons" and "twice read in each House but [it] is much doubted it will pass."[2]

But the act did pass in early May. By that time, Caswell had run for reelection as governor but had been defeated by Alexander Martin. Initially, he had written to his son William that he was going to withdraw his candidacy before the "day of the election." Furthermore, if his salary as comptroller was reduced by the assembly, as he anticipated, he would "resign [as senator and comptroller], and be at liberty to follow my own pursuits in which case I think to visit the western waters."[3] In the end, however, he stood for election and was defeated by a vote of sixty-six to forty-nine in the assembly. Martin supporters—led by Archibald Maclaine, a leading politician from Wilmington—accused Caswell of being "a man who had basely abandoned his important trusts, and deserted his colors in the hour of distress." According to Martin biographer Charles D. Rodenbough, Maclaine "employed the ultimate political weapon of the time by charging Caswell with undefined courageous shortcomings—apparently with reference to his hurried retreat after the debacle at Camden and his subsequent resignation from command of the state militia."[4]

The selection of the next governor became a bit complicated when the assembly convened in another session in November 1784 and—not waiting

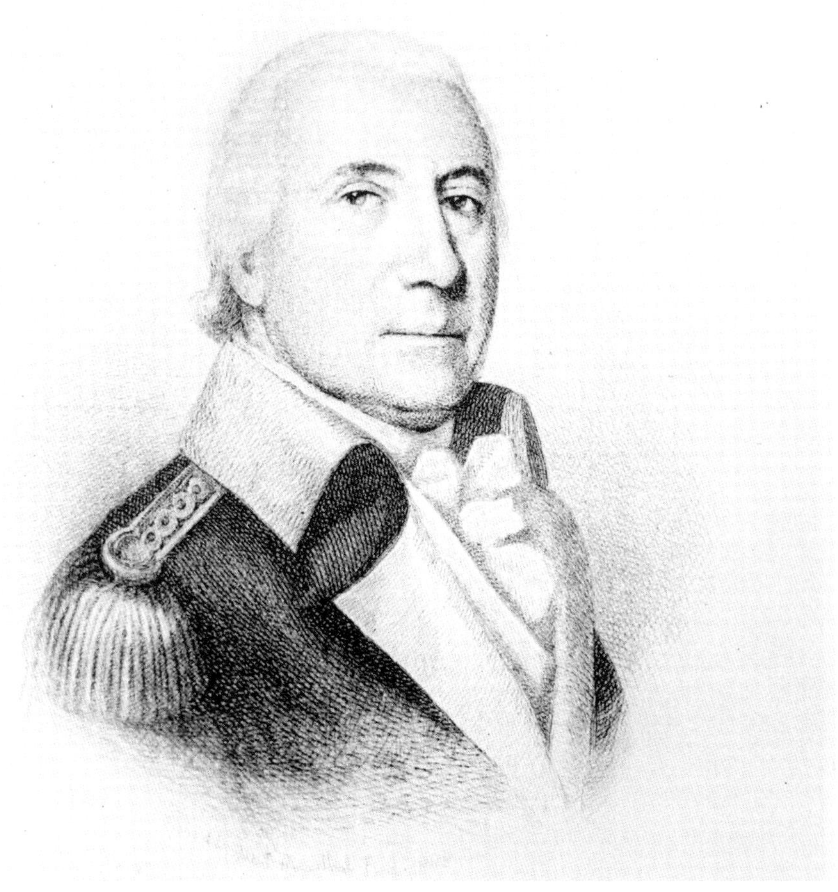

Governor Alexander Martin.

for the customary spring session in 1785 to vote for a governor for the new year—reelected Caswell by a large majority. Abner Nash was the defeated candidate. But Martin's term as chief executive was not scheduled to end until the next May. Thus, for six months, "North Carolina had a governor and a governor elect," with Caswell "functioning as Speaker of the Senate."[5] Then, on May 13, 1785, Caswell's ceremony of installation as governor took place at Tower Hill, near his home at Kinston. In his inaugural address, Speaker of the House William Blount praised Caswell and presented him with a "sword as an emblem of power and authority."[6]

Meanwhile, in the previous autumn, North Carolina had repealed its Cession Act, in part because—as argued by William R. Davie and others

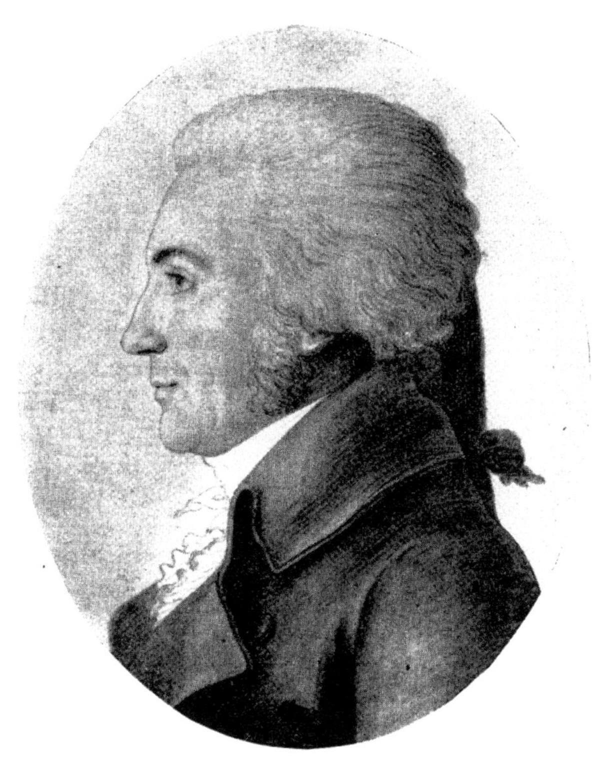

William R. Davie.

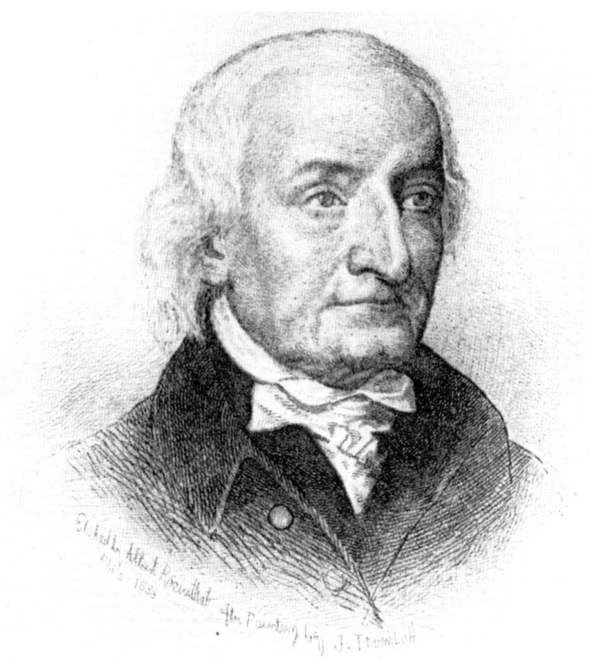

Hugh Williamson.

in the state legislature—North Carolina's share of the war debt had not been determined. Hugh Williamson, in the Confederation Congress, opposed the act because it did not provide "adequate protection to North Carolina." Consequently, when Caswell took office in 1785, he had to deal with problems that had arisen with settlers in the western territories, who had established their own government known as the State of Franklin, with John Sevier as governor. Many white settlers in the West supported the establishment of Franklin because they believed the new state would serve their interests—including land claims and protection from Indian attack—better than the government of North Carolina, dominated by eastern political power. However, before he left office, Governor Martin had declared the people of Franklin in revolt and demanded that they disband their government and renew their allegiance to North Carolina. For Martin, the creation of the State of Franklin violated North Carolina's sovereignty.[7]

Sevier refused to comply with Martin's manifesto, and on May 14, 1785, he wrote to Caswell explaining his refusal and what he considered the injustice of Martin's demand. "Governor Martin," he complained, "have [*sic*] lately sent up to our Country a Manifesto, together with letters to private persons, in order to stir up Sedition and Insurrection thinking thereby to destroy that peace and tranquillity which has [*sic*] so greatly subsisted among the peaceful citizens of the Country." He went on to explain to Caswell that the State of Franklin had been formed while the Cession Act was still in effect. That act, he said, "declared to the world, that this Country was ceded off to Congress. And one part of the Express conditions was, that the same should be erected into one or more states. And we believed that Body was candid, and that they fully believed a new State would tend to the mutual advantage of all parties—that they were as well acquainted with our circumstances at that time, as Governor Martin can be since." As to Martin's claim that the creation of Franklin was an unlawful revolt against North Carolina, Sevier argued that "if Governor Martin is right in his suggestion, we can only say the Assembly of No. Carolina deceived us." Westerners who established Franklin, he maintained, were following the law as it existed at the time—that is, before the Cession Act was repealed. "Therefore we can by no means think it can be called a revolt, or known by such a name."[8]

Apparently, in large part swayed by Sevier's argument, Caswell took a more conciliatory approach than Martin had in dealing with the western settlers who wanted an independent state, thereby avoiding the armed conflict beyond the mountains between North Carolina and Franklin that might have ensued under Martin. Of course, with his vast western landholdings,

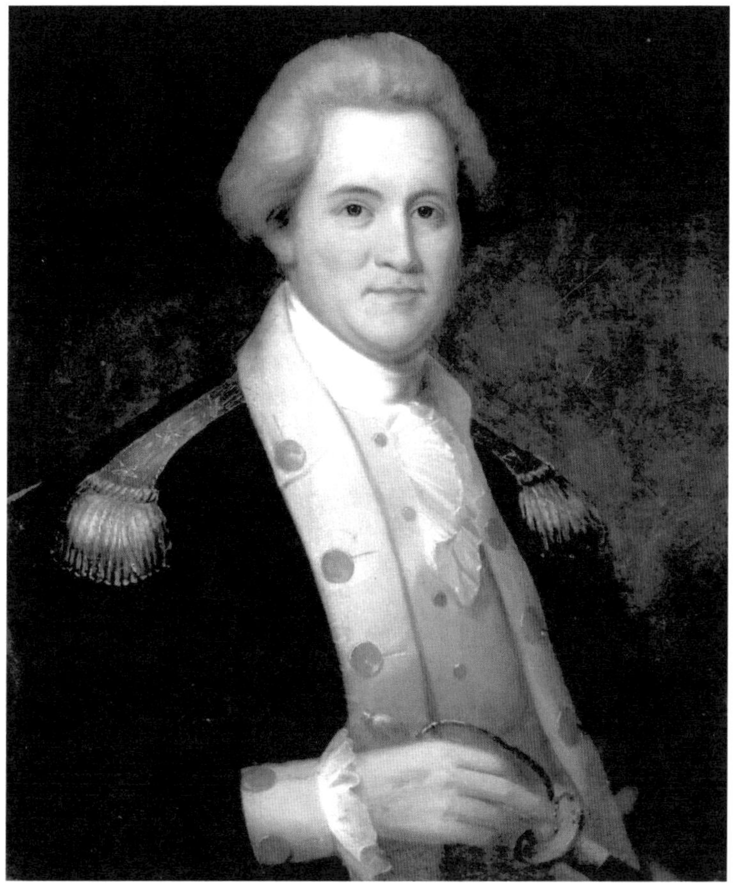

John Sevier.

Caswell had an economic interest in Franklin, as well as a close relationship with Sevier. The legislature of Franklin had even named one of its four new counties for him. Caswell, therefore, did not force the issue of having the State of Franklin terminate but instead bided his time to seek a solution, after conferring with the state's delegates to the Confederation Congress. In the meantime, he and his friend Sevier continued to speculate in land in Greene County.[9]

Sevier also pointed out to him that the western settlers had formed their own government partly for mutual protection against the Cherokee, who had killed forty whites following the cession. The Indians were revolting against seizure of their lands and attacks by whites. They demanded compensation for the loss of their lands, and Caswell agreed to Sevier's request to send goods and supplies to appease the Indians.[10] In early 1785, Caswell had informed the state's delegates to Congress about the persistent problem of violence between whites and the Cherokee in the West. He reported that he had

> *sent a Talk to the Cherokees, expressive of our friendship . . . and requiring that they forbear all acts of hostility—that an inquiry will be made into the wrongs, at the treaty in April next, and a redress endeavored to be made, tho' this is almost impossible as our people are daily offending them and trespassing on their lands. I am doubtful they will be influenced by the ill disposition of the Northern Indians who have lately been tampering with them, to urge them for war. I have not heard how Congress succeeded in their treaties with the Northern tribes.*[11]

On May 31, 1785, Sevier signed a treaty "at the mouth of Dumplin Creek on French Broad River" with Aucoo, chief of Chota, and other chiefs of Cherokee towns. The agreement assigned to whites Cherokee lands "lying and being on the South side of Holeson and French Broad Rivers, as far South as the ridge that divides the Waters of Little River from the Waters of Tenesse."[12] But the Confederation Congress had not recognized the State of Franklin and sought to maintain peaceful relations with the Cherokee. It therefore nullified Sevier's Treaty of Dumplin Creek. The Congress's commissioners—Benjamin Hawkins, Joseph Martin and Andrew Pickens—then negotiated a new treaty. By the time the Treaty of Hopewell was signed at Pickens's South Carolina plantation on November 28, 1785, land-greedy settlers had already crossed the boundary line into Indian territory.[13]

Conflict with the Native American tribes on the frontier beyond the mountains continued as whites persisted in infringing on Indian lands, and both sides committed atrocities. As speculators still sought to grab the Muscle Shoals tract in 1785 and 1786, the Creek Indians, led by Chief Alexander McGillivray, an educated man of mixed blood, attempted to drive them off. During the conflict, Caswell refused to intervene on behalf of the whites, and he expressed sympathy for the Indians. He informed McGillivray that the government of North Carolina was "concerned that any citizen of this State should have given your people any just cause of Complaint by their encroachments upon the Hunting grounds of the Creek Nation." He assured the chief that "nothing shall be done under the authority of the State respecting your people but shall be strictly Consistent with the Ties of Friendship." As the Creeks maintained their attacks on encroaching whites, Caswell initially declined requests to send troops to help suppress the

Indians. Then, in late 1786, the Franklin "land jobbers" formed an alliance with the State of Georgia to campaign against the Creeks, who, in response, expanded their assaults on white settlers.[14]

In 1787, Colonel James Robertson, a leader of the Franklin settlement of Cumberland, appealed to Caswell to dispatch North Carolina militia to battle the Indians. According to Robertson, the Spanish were encouraging the Creeks to attack white settlements, supplying them with ammunition and offering them rewards for American scalps. In February, the North Carolina Assembly had authorized Caswell to send a detachment of militia over the mountains. But the troops, commanded by Major Thomas Evans, did not arrive until October, having endured many delays and hardships en route. In November, Evans reported to the governor about clashes with the Indians and the number of white settlers killed or wounded in the vicinity of Nashville and the Red River. Caswell reassured Chief McGillivray that the North Carolina militia had been dispatched over the mountains merely for defense of settlers and not to initiate war. He reemphasized that his government was concerned about white settlers' encroachment on Creek lands and expressed his hope that the Indians would seek reconciliation with whites in the West.[15]

Although conflict might have subsided for a time, any reconciliation between the Creeks and Georgia did not hold, as whites' thirst for Indian land continued to grow. Then, in the summer of 1790, the Creeks—to ensure protection of as much of their land as they could—signed a treaty with the federal government, which after the ratification of the United States Constitution claimed jurisdiction over treaties with Native Americans. Chief McGillivray and twenty-seven other chiefs traveled to the national capital, then in New York, where they attended official dinners and festivities prior to the signing. Under the terms of the agreement, known as the Treaty of New York, the Creeks ceded to Georgia two-thirds of the territory claimed by the state at that time in exchange for control over the remaining Indian land and federal guarantee of that tract. But a bribed and corrupt Georgia legislature quickly overturned the treaty, and land speculators, calling themselves the Yazoo Company, began grabbing up millions of acres of what is now much of the states of Tennessee, Alabama and Mississippi. The federal government failed to intercede and enforce the Indians' rights according to the Treaty of New York.[16]

The same fate befell the Cherokee in their attempts to form lasting treaties. In the summer of 1786, the Cherokee resumed their raids on white settlements, as settlers persisted in pushing onto their lands. Sevier led a militia expedition in retaliation against the Indians, burning several villages and killing a number of natives. The bloodshed continued as the Indians raided and whites launched preemptive strikes against them. As the violence raged, Caswell gave his approval to the attacks by the Franklinite militia. Gaining the upper hand in the fighting, the Franklin government finally forced the Cherokee into signing the Treaty of Coytee, telling them that "it was your Faults that we come out to War. We have a right to all the ground we marched over." The new state then opened a land office and began selling to whites vast tracts of land that included many Cherokee towns. Treaties, however, did not end the bloody violence between whites and the Cherokee beyond the mountains. Both sides still committed atrocities and massacres until the State of Franklin ended in March 1788. The federal government subsequently initiated a treaty with the Cherokee after North Carolina ceded its western territory to the United States government.[17]

With the Treaty of Holston at Knoxville in July 1791, Congress, under the authority of the United States Constitution, established further borders and provided for the federal government's supervision of future relations with the Cherokee. William Blount of North Carolina, then governor of the Southwest Territory and superintendent of the Southern District, negotiated and signed the agreement with the Cherokee nation. But that treaty would not hold either. Georgia continued to press for jurisdiction over the Creeks, Cherokee and other southern tribes. At the same time, the federal government increasingly acquiesced to a gradual Indian displacement that would end in President Andrew Jackson's Indian Removal Act of 1830, which authorized the forcible removal of the southern tribes to west of the Mississippi River.[18]

Long before that, of course, the State of Franklin had ceased to exist. In fact, its existence had always been tenuous. Settlers in the West had not been unanimous in support for the independent state. A faction led by John Tipton opposed separation from North Carolina and the efforts by Sevier's followers to establish a constitution and government for Franklin.[19] As the conflict continued and the possibility of violence loomed, Caswell called for calm and reconciliation between the two factions. In a May 1787 proclamation to the people in the West, he urged them to end their quarreling and thus avoid armed intervention by the state of North Carolina. He used the threat of Indian attacks as an incentive for the two sides to cease arguing and unite against a common foe. "You have, or shortly will have if my information is well grounded," he told them, "enemies to deal with which may require this cement to be more strong than ever; your whole force may become necessary to be exerted against the common enemy as 'tis more than probable they may be assisted by the subjects of some foreign power [the Spanish], if not publicly they will furnish arms and ammunition privately to the Indian tribes to be made use of against you, and when your neighbors are so supported and assisted by the Northern and Southern Indians, if you should be so unhappy as to be divided among yourselves what may you not then apprehend? I dread the event."

To those who wanted a new state in the West, he held out the reassurance that if they abandoned the current struggle for an independent Franklin and accepted the lawful repeal of the Cession Act, a new state would soon follow anyway. "The General Assembly have told you," he declared,

> *whenever your wealth and numbers so much increase as to make a separation necessary they will be willing* [that] *the same shall take place upon Friendly & reciprocal Terms. . . . If that is the case must not every thinking man believe that this separation will be soonest and most effectually obtained by unanimity. Let that carry you to the quiet submission to the Laws of No. Carolina, till your numbers will justify a General application & then I have no doubt but the same may be obtained upon the principles held out by the Assembly, nay 'tis my opinion that it may be obtained at an earlier day than some imagine, if unanimity prevailed amongst you.*

Caswell emphasized, however, that the people in the West should not think that his conciliatory advice implied that he would not use military force if lawlessness and violence occurred in the region. He cautioned that

> *if you do you may repent it when 'tis too late, when the Blood of some of your dearest and worthiest Citizens may have been spilt and your Country laid waste in an unnatural and Cruel Civil War, and you Cannot suppose, if such an event should take place, that* [the] *Government will supinely look on and see you Cutting each other's throats without interfering and exerting her powers to reduce the disobedient.*[20]

Along with Caswell's carrot-and-stick advice came promises by the North Carolina legislature to remit taxes owed by westerners and to give pardons to any separatists. Without revenue to support itself, and with a new United States Constitution and government in the offing, the temporary State of Franklin collapsed on March 3, 1788. In 1789, North Carolina ceded its western lands to the United States government. In 1794, the Territory of

Tennessee was formed from those lands, and two years later the state of Tennessee joined the Union.[21]

The difficulties involving western lands were just one indication of the dilemma that the new United States faced because its central government lacked the means and power to address pressing issues on a national scale. The Articles of Confederation, adopted by the Continental Congress in November 1771 and ratified by the states in March 1781, became the basis on which Congress would govern the nation. However, the document gave little power to that body, leaving it unable to accomplish those measures normally carried out by an effective government. Under the Articles, Congress remained subservient to the state governments and could do little without their authorization. The Articles did not provide for an executive or national court system, nor did they allow Congress to levy taxes to pay the nation's debts or to regulate domestic and foreign commerce, except with the Indians. Congress could conduct foreign policy, but any treaties it negotiated or laws it passed required the approval of nine of the thirteen states.[22] "By the end of the war," writes historian Robert Middlekauff, "the inadequacy of the Articles was clear. Yet through much of the 1780s, they could not be revised. They could not because the Americans were unable to find a way to reconcile local attachments with centralized government."[23]

The inadequacy of the Confederation government to enforce the terms of the 1783 peace treaty worried Caswell as postwar governor, and he voiced his concern and advice to the Congress. In the treaty, Britain agreed to evacuate its military outposts on the western frontier. But that country continued to occupy posts in the Northwest, particularly along the Great Lakes, in order to exploit the fur trade in that region. Spain would not acknowledge the claims of the United States to the region between Florida and the Ohio River and attempted to close the Mississippi River to American commerce.[24] The Confederation government remained powerless to address those problems. Like other leaders, Caswell was annoyed and angered by the situation. He advised Congress to demand that the British relinquish outposts on the Lakes or face military action. "Permit me to suggest," he wrote to the delegates on January 20, 1785, "that a remonstrance should be made to the Court of Britain requiring their reasons for this infraction of the treaty—should they not be satisfactory, an Army ought to be raised and these Posts attempted to be taken by force. A manifesto ought also to be published to the World explaining the reasons for so doing." But realizing his call for military action might be premature and rash, he tempered his advice. "However," he concluded, "this business requires prudence, caution

& address which I make no doubt will be made use of by the Honourable body, of which you are a member."[25]

Yet another difficulty that the postwar United States government had with Britain and other countries was establishing equitable trade laws and other international agreements. In an effort to keep the new nation "weak and dependent," European countries imposed "harsh trade restrictions and rebuffed appeals for concessions."[26] Britain refused even to send a minister to the United States to negotiate trade and other agreements.[27] Caswell recognized the inequity of trade laws that favored Britain over the United States, and he supported the retaliatory measure of having the states themselves levy duties on British shipping. With his endorsement, the General Assembly, in November 1785, placed a duty of five shillings per ton on vessels from other countries trading with North Carolina. The state's lawmakers also raised North Carolina's tariff on manufactured goods imported from overseas.[28]

The British government countered American complaints with charges of its own that some of the states were not observing the peace treaty of 1783 and were in fact passing acts in violation of its terms. The Confederation Congress had difficulty getting the states to comply with the terms of the treaty. Ultimately, in April 1787, Arthur St. Clair, president of the Confederation Congress, wrote to Caswell that "we have deliberately and dispassionately examined and Considered the several facts & Matters urged by Britain as infractions of the Treaty of Peace on the Part of America, and we regret that in some of the States too little attention appears to have been paid to the Faith Pledged by that Treaty." He reminded the governor that the Articles of Confederation (in Article 9) gave to Congress "the sole and exclusive right & power of determining war & peace and entering into Treaties and Alliances &c." And "when therefore a Treaty is Constitutionally made, Ratified and Published by us, it immediately becomes binding on the whole nation and Superadded to the Laws of the Land without the interventions of State Legislatures." Consequently, any acts passed by a state legislature in violation of the 1783 treaty should be repealed.

St. Clair did not specifically accuse North Carolina of enacting laws that injured the nation's relations with Britain and usurped congressional authority. Congress's "Resolution," he told Caswell, "applies strictly only to such of the States as have passed the exceptionable Acts alluded to." Nevertheless, Congress was stipulating that "every state without exception"—whether or not it had violated the Treaty of 1783—must enact a law that prohibited any legislation that ran contrary to the treaty and jeopardized relations between Britain and the United States. He called on Caswell to request "without delay" that North Carolina's General Assembly pass such an act and transmit a copy to Congress. That measure would reassure Britain of the nation's commitment to the terms of the treaty and lead to the final evacuation of British outposts on the United States frontier. "It certainly is time," declared St. Clair,

> *that all doubts respecting the Public faith be removed and that all questions & differences between us & Great Britain be removed and finally settled. The States are informed of the reasons why his Britannic Majesty still continues to occupy the frontier post which by the Treaty he agreed to evacuate and we have the strongest assurances that an exact compliance with the Treaty on our part shall be followed by a punctual performance of it on the part of Great Britain.*[29]

Although annoyed by Britain's inequitable trade arrangements, Caswell concurred with Congress's position about adhering to the terms of the peace treaty and maintaining good relations with Britain. He responded to St. Clair in early June that he would "take the earliest opportunity in my power of laying before the Legislature of this State" the request for the specified act and said that he had "not the smallest fear but the importance of the subject with the cogent reasons assigned by Congress would have proper weight with that Assembly and produce the desired effect." As Caswell predicted, the General Assembly passed legislation endorsing the treaty.[30]

But as Caswell and other American leaders were beginning to conclude, the problematic trade relations, along with the persistent and defiant British presence in the Northwest and the problem—without unified authority—of ensuring the compliance of the states with treaty obligations were serious indications that the federal government under the Articles of Confederation lacked the power to establish a national foreign policy that would enable the United States to compete with European countries on a global scale. "More than anything else," asserts foreign affairs historian George C. Herring, "their inability to effectively address crucial foreign policy problems persuaded many leaders that a stronger central government was essential to the nation's survival."[31]

Caswell expressed his frustration at the difficulty of something so fundamental as getting the state's delegates—appointed by the General Assembly—even to attend the sessions of Congress. Some prominent appointees, such as Samuel Johnston and John Sitgraves (Caswell's aide at the Battle of Camden), refused to serve. Richard Dobbs Spaight and Timothy Bloodworth accepted appointments but soon resigned. William Blount informed the governor that he would serve only if he were paid in hard currency. Caswell pointed out to the legislature that a major obstacle in getting delegates to attend Congress was the state's failure to pay their salaries and expenses adequately. Frequently, delegates from other states also did not attend Congress, and sometimes a quorum could not be convened. Without the demands of war that drew the states together to act in union, it seemed that cooperation among the states was collapsing and that the very existence of Congress and the possibility of a strong American Republic were in jeopardy. Governor Benjamin Harrison of Virginia remarked that during the war, "the eyes of the world were upon us, and we were the wonder and envy of all," but at present, "we are sinking faster in esteem than we arose."[32]

In January 1786, Virginia extended an invitation to the states to send delegates to a convention in September in Annapolis, Maryland, to consider how to improve the regulation of commerce on a national scale. Caswell received notification of the planned convention in a March letter from Massachusetts governor James Bowdoin, along "with a copy of a Resolution of the Legislature of the Commonwealth of Massachusetts aceeding [*sic*] to the proposal of Virginia for holding at Annapolis in Maryland a Convention of Delegates from the Several States in the Union for the Purpose of considering the Trade of the United States." He informed the Massachusetts governor on June 21 that "as the Time appointed for the meeting of the General Assembly of this State is Subsequent to the first Monday in September, the Council have advised me to appoint Commissioners" to attend the Annapolis conference. The commissioners recommended by Caswell were "the Honorable Abner Nash esquire, Alfred Moore, Hugh Williamson, John G. Blount, and Philemon Hawkins, esquires or any two of them." Caswell agreed that "the appointment will be accordingly made of such of these Gentlemen who shall agree to attend."[33] Of the five appointees, only Williamson accepted the assignment, and he arrived in Annapolis after the convention had adjourned. But North Carolina was not the sole state that did not have attending delegates. Only New York, New Jersey, Pennsylvania, Delaware and Virginia sent commissioners. Even Maryland, the host state, was not represented.[34]

Although the main purpose of the meeting was to deal with trade relations, New Jersey delegates carried instructions to consider "other matters." Yet with only five of the states represented, it became obvious that little could be decided, and the delegates disbanded. But by that time, a movement had begun among the members—led by Alexander Hamilton of New York, James Madison of Virginia and the New Jersey delegation—to revise the Articles of Confederation significantly. Therefore, before it dissolved, the convention called on the states to appoint commissioners to convene again in 1787 "to take into consideration the situation of the United States, to devise such further provisions as shall appear to them necessary to render the constitution of the Federal government adequate to the exigencies of the Union."[35]

By that time, Caswell and other like-minded political leaders in the state and nation had come to the full realization that the Articles of Confederation would not do for an emerging republic striving to survive, compete and prosper in an expanding, modern and largely monarchical world. The individual state constitutions would not suffice for unified action. A new system of national governance had to be developed. "If it were not," writes historian Robert Middlekauff, "a confederacy of small sovereign republics, a radical institution in a world of monarchies, might collapse or be conquered." Governor Harrison of Virginia opined that the nations of Europe were poised "like buzzards to feast on the spoils of our demise."[36] Such was the dilemma facing the delegates from North Carolina who, in May 1787, gathered in Philadelphia with representatives from the other states to consider the future of the United States government.

In its 1786–87 session, the North Carolina General Assembly, with reluctance by some members, had endorsed the revision of the Articles of Confederation. Although Caswell and his conservative allies in the General Assembly embraced revision, a strong element in the legislature opposed the idea of establishing a stronger central government, which might threaten individual liberties. That opposition came largely from the class of small farmers in the backcountry. After considerable debate, the state lawmakers, on January 6, the last day of the legislative session, appointed delegates to attend the coming convention in Philadelphia. The North Carolina legislators' decision to send representatives to the convention resulted in large measure from the efforts of Caswell, who urged their compliance, citing a letter from Virginia's governor calling for "zealous attention to the present American crisis."[37]

For Caswell—as for such leaders of the Revolution as Washington, Adams, Franklin, Hamilton, Madison and John Jay—creating a strong nation in the aftermath of the war for independence was as necessary and challenging as was a battlefield victory. Otherwise, the Revolution would be incomplete, and the armed struggle would ultimately prove to have been in vain. Only a new, strong federal republic—rather than the present loose confederation of states, each with its own agenda—could provide the national strength and leadership to fulfill the promise of the American Revolution. Although, when considering the future of the Confederation, Caswell and his like might not have been full-blown nationalists, they (including Jefferson) realized the importance of collective action by the thirteen states if the experiment of an American Republic was to succeed. They saw that without sufficient power invested in a federal government, dissolution awaited the burgeoning nation.

In supporting a convention to develop a stronger central government, Caswell was joined in North Carolina by other leading men of his class, men who shared common concerns about both their and the nation's futures. These upper-class North Carolinians saw a strong national government as necessary for the survival of the new nation but also as a protector of their own power and prosperity and as a bulwark against such political and social instability as had arisen in the Regulator movement. According to historian A.R. Newsome, the General Assembly's decision

> *to participate in the convention was due to the political skill and activity of Governor Richard Caswell, William R. Davie, John Gray Blount, Richard Dobbs Spaight, Archibald Maclaine, and other leaders of a small group of upper-class eastern conservatives, primarily from the plantation, slaveholding, and commercial Cape Fear, Roanoke, and Albemarle–Pamlico Sound regions of the east, whose interests were threatened by the prevailing bankruptcy, commercial chaos, and excess of democratic local self-government.*[38]

The North Carolina delegates selected to attend the convention in Philadelphia were William R. Davie, Willie Jones, Alexander Martin, Richard Dobbs Spaight and Caswell, despite the legislature's having just reelected him governor. Caswell, however, declined to attend because of ill health. Jones turned down the appointment because he objected to establishing a central government that would be stronger than the one provided for in the Articles of Confederation. Caswell was authorized to fill the two vacancies, and he chose Hugh Williamson and William Blount.[39] Caswell and these men agreed about government's role in protecting liberty and property and ensuring social and economic stability. According to one excellent general description,

The North Carolina delegates were from the upper social and economic class—well educated for their day, conservative in political, social, and economic outlook, experienced in public life as successful planters, lawyers, and businessmen, representing the best life of the state and qualified by native intelligence and training to represent the state in the convention. Their average age was a little less than forty, ranging from Davie's thirty to Williamson's fifty-one. Davie, Martin, and Williamson were college graduates. All five had served in the Revolution, Davie with distinction. Davie was a prominent attorney and planter, owner of thirty-six slaves; Blount, a merchant, planter, businessman, owner of thirty slaves; Martin, a lawyer and planter, owner of forty-seven slaves; Spaight, a wealthy planter, owner of seventy-one slaves; Williamson, a physician, merchant, and businessman. All but Martin had served in the Congress of the Confederation and Martin had been governor and judge. But none of the five had had experience in constitution-making. All but Martin were from the East, and no one of the five represented, in personal status, opinions, background, or interest, the small farmer class that constituted the majority of the state's population.[40]

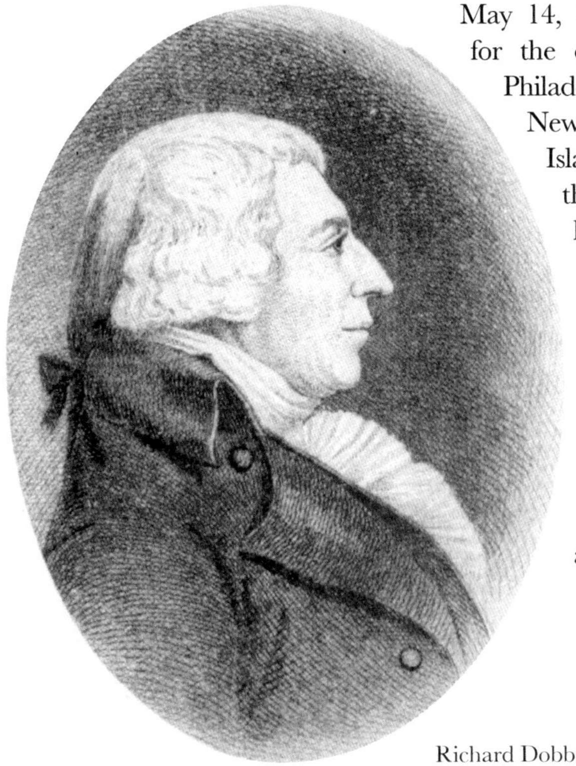

May 14, 1787, became the day set for the convention to convene in Philadelphia, and all states except New Hampshire and Rhode Island had elected delegates by then. When that date arrived, however, only Virginia and Pennsylvania were present at Philadelphia's statehouse (Independence Hall). Finally, on May 25, a quorum of seven states opened the convention. In a short while, all the states except New Hampshire and Rhode Island had

Richard Dobbs Spaight.

representatives on hand. New Hampshire would send delegates in July, but Rhode Island did not attend.[41]

The first question facing the convention was whether the Articles of Confederation should be revised or an entirely new constitution written, which document would provide for a central government powerful enough to impose collective national policies on the states and their citizens. By May 30, the decision had been made to prepare an entirely new document. But as historian Gordon S. Wood has noted, "It was not the defects of the Articles of Confederation" only that led to the decision to draft a new constitution. "The defects were correctable," he claims. What many of the early political leaders, including Caswell, had come to fear was that the new, powerful state legislatures posed a threat to individual liberties and effective government. "By the 1780s," writes Wood, "it seemed as if the majorities of the popular legislatures had become just as dangerous to individual liberties as the detested royal governors had been." A strong central government was therefore needed to protect fundamental rights and curb the abuses against liberty imposed by state legislatures "backed by the bulk of the electorates in each state." After the war with Britain, a number of the nation's founders "had come to realize that the Revolution had unleashed social and political forces that they had not anticipated and that the 'excess of democracy' threatened the very essence of their republican revolution." Even Thomas Jefferson, the premier spokesman for state and individual rights and a limited national government, acknowledged that "173 despots would surely be as oppressive as one" and that "an elective despotism was not the government we fought for."[42] Jefferson also conceded the right and obligation of the Confederation to compel an individual state to conduct its affairs in the collective interests of the union of states. "When any one state in the American Union refuses obedience to the Confederation by which they have bound themselves," he proclaimed in 1786, "the rest have a natural right to compel them to obedience."[43]

James Madison of Virginia emerged as a chief force for writing a constitution that would provide for a strong central government composed of executive, judicial and legislative branches. Edmund Randolph, also from Virginia, would present to the convention Madison's Virginia Plan for the establishment of such a government. Four days after opening, the convention elected George Washington as chairman. Throughout the convention, the influential Washington, hero of the Revolution, actively supported the creation of a strong nationalist government. The delegates gathered at

Philadelphia were some of the nation's most capable political leaders. In addition to Madison, Washington and Randolph, other delegates from Virginia included George Wythe and George Mason. From Pennsylvania came Benjamin Franklin, Gouverneur Morris and James Wilson. New York sent Alexander Hamilton. John Dickinson and George Read came from Delaware, and William Paterson led the New Jersey delegation. Massachusetts was represented by Elbridge Gerry, Rufus King and Nathaniel Gorham. South Carolina had present John Rutledge, Charles Cotesworth Pinckney, Charles Pinckney and Pierce Butler. Maryland dispatched the talkative and tiresome Luther Martin.[44]

Among such an able body of men, the North Carolina delegation did not stand out or make a large contribution to the composition of the Constitution. William Blount, who also served as a member of the Confederation Congress meeting in New York, was absent from Philadelphia for much of the time. He did not make any speeches or serve on any committees. Neither did Martin. Davie made several speeches and was on the committee that produced the "Great Compromise," which reconciled the conflict between small and large states about representation in Congress. Spaight made a number of speeches, motions and seconds. He also proposed two provisions of the Constitution: the election of United States senators by the state legislatures and the authorization of the president to make appointments when Congress was in recess. Unlike the other North Carolina delegates, however, he opposed the Great Compromise. Hugh Williamson, the primary spokesman for his delegation, rose as the most influential and active North Carolinian in the drafting of the Constitution. He delivered seventy-three speeches and twenty-three motions and voiced thirteen seconds. He served on five committees. The convention adopted his proposal for a six-year term for United States senators, and he made several important suggestions regarding the impeachment of the president, the federal census and electoral apportionment.

The North Carolina delegation supported the Three-fifths Compromise, which allowed each slaveholding state to count a slave as three-fifths of a person in determining its number of representatives in the United States House and in apportioning its taxes. The North Carolina delegates also endorsed compromises that postponed for twenty years the abolition of the foreign slave trade and disallowed the taxing of exports. They adamantly opposed the establishment of an executive, or president, independent of Congress who could be reelected to office. They voted with the other large states for having representation in the national government based on population but objected to letting future states enter the union on an equal basis with the existing states. However, they approved of authorizing Congress to admit new states.[45]

Caswell encouraged North Carolina delegates in their responsibilities at Philadelphia, including securing allowances for them from the state treasury, although he did not attempt to dictate how they voted on issues. In the final weeks of the convention, he urged them to stay the course, put their personal business at home on hold and see the work through to the end. "Your task," he wrote, "is arduous and requires time for deliberation and consideration. But the future happiness of the State depends so much on the convention that I know you will complete the work if possible, though it costs you your own interests. I shall be happy to render or to receive advice from you."[46]

Caswell did, however, show concern when he did not hear about the progress of the convention from the delegates, although he accepted their explanation that all the members had pledged to keep the negotiations as secret as possible until the final document had been drafted.[47] Caswell also made known to the delegates his position favoring the creation of a strong national government and his preference that that government be centered on three separate branches of governance: legislative, executive and judicial. In late July, as the convention neared completion of its work, he wrote to Spaight:

> *I am induced to think that the plan of a National Parliament and Supreme Executive with adequate powers to the Government of the Union will be more suitable to our situation & circumstances than any other, but I should wish also an independent Judicial department to decide any contest that may happen between the United States and individual States & between one State and another; this however is only a hint, you may not see the necessity of it as forcible as I do and I presume 'tis now too late to offer any reasons for the establishment, as that matter I flatter myself is before this got over; all I can say respecting the Convention is to recommend a perseverence to the end, to the deputies from this State.*[48]

The delegates in Philadelphia did, indeed, persevere until they produced a Constitution approved by the convention, although the process was laborious and filled with debate and disagreement, without an abundance of precedent to guide them. On June 14, North Carolina's delegates (except Blount with Congress in New York) had reported to Caswell on the meeting's progress and the difficulty of resolving the question of state versus central authority. They wrote:

> *By the date of this* [letter] *you will observe we are near the middle of June and though we sit from day to day, Saturdays included, it is not possible for us to determine when the business before us can be finished, a very large Field presents to our view without a single Straight or eligible Road that has been trodden by the feet of Nations. An Union of Sovereign States, preserving their Civil Liberties and connecting together by such Tyes as to Preserve permanent & effective Governments is a system not described, it is a Circumstance that has not Occurred in the History of men; if we shall be so fortunate as to find this in descript our Time will have been well spent. Several members of the Convention have their Wives here and other Gentlemen have sent for theirs. This Seems to promise a Summer's Campaign. Such of us as can remain here from the inevitable avocation of private business, are resolved to Continue whilst there is any Prospect of being able to serve the State & Union.*[49]

Ultimately, argument and compromise ended, and the convention had drafted the Constitution of the United States for the delegates' signatures. Not all agreed to sign it. Dissatisfied with some of its provisions, George Mason and Edmund Randolph of Virginia and Elbridge Gerry of Massachusetts refused to sign. Some delegates (fifty-five attended at various times) left the convention before the vote for ratification because they objected to the establishment of a strong central government. Among them were John Lansing and Robert Yates of New York, who departed Philadelphia on July 10, leaving their state without a quorum, although Hamilton signed the Constitution anyway. Rhode Island never attended the convention, thereby making the final vote eleven to none for approval. Three of the five North Carolina delegates signed—Williamson, Spaight and Blount. By the time the signing took place on September 17, Davie and Martin had returned to North Carolina but supported the signing.[50]

In late August, Martin had informed Caswell that the work of the convention was nearing completion. Davie, he wrote, had departed Philadelphia "under the Necessity to return Home," and "I am also obliged to be at Salisbury Superior Court in Sept. next." Blount, meanwhile, had journeyed from New York to Philadelphia for final negotiations and signing of the Constitution. Martin reassured the governor that they were unanimous in support of the new document. Even though he would not be present for further discussion and signing, he told Caswell that

> *the State will still be represented fully in Convention by my Honourable friends Messrs. Spaight, Blount & Williamson. My absence may I think be the more easily dispenced with when I have the pleasure to inform your Excellency the Deputation from the State of North Carolina have generally been unanimous on all great questions, and I flatter myself will continue so until the Objects of their mission be finished.*

Again, he acknowledged that the delegates were under a gag order not to reveal to the public the work of the convention until it was completed. He did, however, go so far as to assuage any fears that Caswell might have had about the forthcoming Constitution's being too conservative or monarchical: "Tho' I have not told your Excellency affirmatively what the Convention have done, I can tell you negatively what they have not done. They are not about to create a King as hath been represented unfavourably in some of the eastern States, so that you are not to expect the Bishop Oznaburg or any prince or great man of the World to rule in this Country." He did not expect it to be long before the new Constitution would be before the North Carolina General Assembly.[51]

Blount also had written to Caswell informing him of his plans to remain in Philadelphia until the Constitution was completed and signed and then to return to Congress in New York. Williamson, too, assured the governor of the remaining delegates' commitment to see their task through to the end because "we owe it to the feelings of your Excellency, for we would not have it alleged that Gentlemen whom you had been pleased to honor with the Public trust had failed in a single Iota of their duty to the Public." Although he could not yet reveal details, he sincerely believed that the efforts of the delegates—at times difficult—had produced a significant document to guide the new nation, and even perhaps the future world. "We shall on some future occasion," he wrote to Caswell, "be at liberty to explain to your Excellency how difficult a part has fallen to the share of our State in the course of this business and I flatter myself greatly . . . [that] we have . . . sustained it with a Principle & firmness that will entitle us to what we will never ask for, the thanks of the public. It will be sufficient for us if we have the satisfaction of believing that we have contributed to the happiness of Millions."[52]

With its work completed, the convention sent the Constitution to Congress for its approval. Congress forwarded copies to the state legislatures without a recommendation. Nine of the thirteen states had to ratify the Constitution in order for it to take effect as the framework for a new federal government.

The state legislatures then called for conventions in which elected delegates would vote for or against ratification.[53] In North Carolina, that process proved difficult.

North Carolinians became bitterly divided over the new Constitution. Members of the upper class, including Caswell, wanted to ratify the document and ensure a strong central government for the nation, which they felt would be supportive of their political ideas and economic interests. These supporters of ratification, called Federalists, were well-to-do planters, lawyers, merchants and Episcopalians who resided largely around the commercial centers in the eastern part of the state. Opponents of ratification, known as Antifederalists, were mostly small, backcountry farmers and religious dissenters who feared that the Constitution would create a powerful national government that would impose heavy taxes and threaten state and individual rights. But as historian William S. Price Jr. has pointed out, "there were notable exceptions to such generalizations in North Carolina, particularly among Antifederalists."[54]

In the ratification movement, North Carolina "lagged far behind" a majority of the other states. It became "the seventh state to call a ratifying convention" and the twelfth to hold a convention, with Rhode Island being the last. The General Assembly called for local elections in March 1788 to select delegates for a convention to convene in Hillsborough. In those local elections, conflict between Federalists and Antifederalists became heated, disruptive and even violent. In Dobbs County, Caswell, whose term as governor had recently ended, was nominated as a Federalist candidate for the upcoming convention. When the Antifederalists carried the vote, the "Federalists knocked over the candles, assaulted the sheriff, and amid the darkness and confusion, made away with the ballot box." The Dobbs Federalists then held a special election—without the Antifederalists—and elected a Federalist delegation, which included Caswell.[55]

When the Hillsborough convention met on July 21, 1788, all the states except North Carolina, Rhode Island and New York had ratified the Constitution (and New York did so on July 26). Because of the irregular Federalist election in Dobbs County, its delegation, which included Caswell and his son Winston, was not seated. At the convention, which met from July 21 until August 4, the delegates passed a resolution "neither to ratify nor reject" the Constitution. The vote in support of the resolution was 184, with 83 in opposition. Having been reelected to the state senate upon leaving the office of governor, Caswell, in November 1788, proposed to the legislature a resolution for convening another convention for ratification. His motion cleared the senate but went down to defeat in the house of commons because of strong opposition by the Antifederalists.[56]

The greatest opposition to the Constitution was based on the fear that an unrestricted central government would threaten individual liberties. Antifederalists argued that such a document should include a guarantee of the rights of the people, a statement similar to the Declaration of Rights in the North Carolina Constitution. As the leading Antifederalist spokesman at Hillsborough, superior court judge Samuel Spencer proclaimed: "The expression, 'We the People of the United States,' shews that this government is intended for individuals; there ought to be a bill of rights." The premier speaker for the Federalists and prominent jurist James Iredell answered in opposition that "a bill of rights, as I conceive, would not only be incongruous, but dangerous. No man, let his ingenuity be what it will, could enumerate all the individual rights not relinquished by this constitution." He argued that any listing of rights would restrict them to the ones actually specified in writing.[57]

After their failure to secure ratification in the summer of 1788, the Federalists changed their position and endorsed the idea of amendments to the Constitution to protect individual freedoms. In June 1789, James Madison submitted for Congress's approval a number of constitutional amendments to serve as a Bill of Rights. A hope of getting North Carolina to ratify was part of his motivation. That shift in policy weakened the resistance of the Antifederalists, who were also beginning to see certain advantages in a strengthened United States government, advantages such as stable currency, military protection and consistent and effective foreign and trade policies. At a second convention held in the "State House" (Old Market House) in Fayetteville on November 16–23, 1789, the delegates decided to ratify the Constitution by a vote of 194 to 77. Ratification of the Bill of Rights (the first ten amendments to the United States Constitution) by the General Assembly soon followed. In 1790, Rhode Island became the last state to ratify the Constitution.[58]

Although he was to be a delegate to the Fayetteville convention, Caswell did not live to see the Constitution ratified. He was serving as Speaker of the state senate when the General Assembly convened in Fayetteville on November 2, two weeks before the ratification convention met in the town. While presiding over the senate on the morning of November 5, Caswell suffered a paralytic stroke, evidently brought on by high blood pressure. He survived for five days at Cool Spring Tavern before dying.

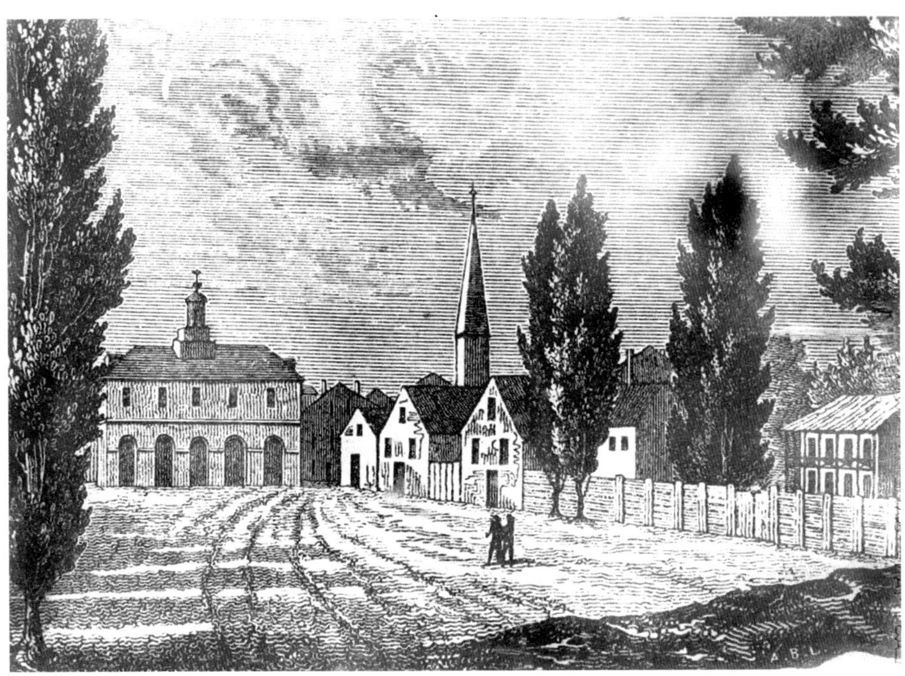

The "State House" (Old Market House) in Fayetteville.

A committee headed by Caswell's friend William Blount, a member of the state senate, was appointed to arrange a funeral procession and service to be attended by members of the General Assembly on November 11. The procession began at "a Church," probably on Cool Spring Street.[59] The order of march was first the clergymen and physicians, followed by the coffin and then the "relatives of the deceased as chief mourners." Next came the members of the senate, two abreast, followed by the members of the house, also "two and two." The governor and then the secretary of state were next in order, followed by the treasurer and comptroller, the clerks of the General Assembly and, finally, other mourners.[60] In November 1788, Caswell had been elected grand master of the North Carolina Grand Lodge of the Most Ancient and Honourable Fraternity of Free and Accepted Masons.[61] Members of the Grand Lodge accompanied the funeral procession "in their masonic dress and order," and the six pallbearers were lodge members as well as members of the General Assembly.[62] The march continued to Market Square, where outdoor eulogies were delivered at the State House while the town bell at Barge's Tavern sounded a dirge. Caswell's body was then transported to Kinston for burial at his Red House plantation.[63]

From Fayetteville on November 22, William Blount wrote to Caswell's nephew William White, "What honors were here paid our old Friend and the Procession was really the most regular I ever saw and I assure you that his death was lamented by all Ranks of People."[64] In New Bern on December 3, "a Funeral Oration . . . was delivered, in Christ Church, before the Right Worshipful the Royal Arch Chapter, St. John's Lodge, a deputation of Kingston and Washington Lodges, and a number of Visiting Brothers. The Gentlemen of the Bar, the Shandean Society, the Newbern Volunteers, and a large concourse of Citizens attended on the occasion."[65]

Caswell's death was preceded by his own considerable grief over the passing of a number of his family members. Between 1784 and 1789, two of his sons, William and Richard Jr., and his eldest daughter, Sarah, died, as did his mother, sister and two brothers. His first wife, Mary Mackilwean Caswell, and son William, who died in 1785, were buried at Red House plantation, but their graves, like his, remain unmarked. His second wife, Sarah Herritage Caswell, died in 1794 at Newington-on-the-Hill and was buried beside her husband in the family cemetery.[66] In addition to her, Caswell was survived by three sons, Winston, Dallam and John, and two daughters, Anna and Susannah. At his death, Caswell was heavily in debt, and most of his estate was eventually liquidated.[67]

Epilogue

Richard Caswell played a vital role in leading North Carolina during the campaign for American independence. Moving to the colony from Maryland at an early age, he quickly established himself as a member of the landed gentry and launched his career in service to the colonial government as a land surveyor, local official, treasurer, militia commander and legislator. Considering himself a loyal subject of the Crown and a proponent of law and order and the protection of property, he supported royal authority as vested in the colonial government, and he led militia troops in the suppression of the backcountry revolt by the Regulators. But as the British government made greater demands on the colonists after the French and Indian War, particularly in levying new taxes, he increasingly rejected royal rule as a threat to Americans' rights and liberty. As the Revolutionary tide swelled throughout the colonies, he came to support independence. By late 1775, colonial governor Josiah Martin was referring to him as "the most active tool of sedition" in North Carolina.

As the movement toward independence grew, Caswell served as a member of North Carolina's Committee of Correspondence and as a delegate to the First and Second Continental Congresses in Philadelphia and to all five of North Carolina's Provincial Congresses. Although he might not have distinguished himself at the Continental Congresses, he exhibited significant leadership at the Provincial Congresses, presiding at the fifth one and acting as chair of the committee that drafted the state's first constitution at that congress. As a major general of militia, he led troops at the Battle of

Moore's Creek Bridge in February 1776. His performance in that fighting helped secure a Patriot victory over a Loyalist force marching to unite with British regulars at the port of Brunswick.

When Caswell was elected the first state governor of North Carolina in 1776, he was immediately inundated with vast wartime responsibilities and problems. Although constrained by his limited powers as chief executive, he exerted considerable effort to fill the ranks of the American army with troops from North Carolina and to keep those soldiers fed and equipped. He also had to contend with the bitter internal struggle between Whigs and Loyalists known as the Tory War. At the same time, he had to respond to conflict between white settlers and Indians in the West and to British raids on the coast. His ability to lead the state under wartime conditions was hindered by the lack of power bestowed on the state's chief executive by the North Carolina Constitution of 1776. In fact, all the new states attempted to limit the gubernatorial powers they had feared and resented under their royal governors. "In their desire to root out tyranny once and for all," writes Gordon Wood, "the members of the state conventions who drafted the new constitutions stripped the new elected governors of much of the power that the royal governors had exercised."[1]

Given the limited powers and difficult circumstances under which he had to govern—particularly in making appointments and obtaining support from the General Assembly—Caswell performed well in his four terms as war governor. He was suffering exhaustion and ill health when he left office in the spring of 1780. Nevertheless, he immediately took the field to command the state militia at the Battle of Camden and went on to serve four years in the state senate, the last as Speaker. Simultaneously, he held the office of comptroller general, with the responsibility of managing state funds amid the financial difficulties of the postwar period.

In 1784, the General Assembly again elected Caswell governor, and he served three consecutive one-year terms, being reelected twice by the legislature. As chief executive once more, he dealt effectively with the crisis over cession of the state's western lands, the temporary State of Franklin and unrest among the Indians. Upon leaving the governor's office in 1787, Caswell was elected as a delegate to the Constitutional Convention in Philadelphia, but he declined to attend because of bad health. As a Federalist, he supported ratification of the United States Constitution. However, as a result of irregularities in his election as a delegate, he was not seated at North Carolina's first convention to consider ratification in Hillsborough in July 1788. But he was returned in 1789 to the senate, where he presided as

Speaker, and was slated to be a delegate at the second state convention for ratification of the Constitution in Fayetteville when he suddenly died.

Richard Caswell's contribution to the cause of American independence was thus substantial. That most of his service was rendered at the state level does not diminish its importance to the revolutionary movement and the founding of the new nation. Caswell might not be remembered as a national Founding Father of the same ilk as Washington, Adams, Franklin or Madison, but as a capable governor and military commander in North Carolina at a time of extreme crisis, he played a significant part in the creation of the republic. It seems unlikely that the nation could have won its independence and forged a new democratic government without the assistance of such state leaders. Years after Caswell's death, President John Adams, firebrand of the American Revolution, reportedly remarked: "We always looked to Richard Caswell for North Carolina. He was a model man and a true patriot."[2]

Notes

Introduction

1. A. Roger Ekirch, *"Poor Carolina": Politics and Society in Colonial North Carolina, 1729–1776* (Chapel Hill: University of North Carolina Press, 1981), 14–17.
2. William S. Price Jr., *"There Ought to Be a Bill of Rights": North Carolina Enters a New Nation* (Raleigh: North Carolina Office of Archives and History, 1991), 13.

Chapter 1

1. *Dictionary of North Carolina Biography*, 6 vols. (Chapel Hill: University of North Carolina Press, 1979–96) s.vv. "Caswell, Richard" and "Caswell, William"; Talmage C. Johnson and Charles R. Holloman, *The Story of Kinston and Lenoir County* (Raleigh, NC: Edwards and Broughton Co., 1954), 34–44. Holloman is the author of the excellent short biographies of the Caswells in the *Dictionary of North Carolina Biography*.
2. *Dictionary of North Carolina Biography*, s.v. "Caswell, Richard"; David Leroy Corbitt, *The Formation of the North Carolina Counties, 1663–1943* (Raleigh: North Carolina Office of Archives and History, 1975), 131, 167.
3. C.B. Alexander, "The Training of Richard Caswell," *North Carolina Historical Review* 23 (January 1946): 13–14. This and two subsequent articles published in the *North Carolina Historical Review* in 1946 were derived from Alexander's "The Public Career of Richard Caswell" (PhD diss., University of North Carolina, 1930).

4. Alexander, "Training of Richard Caswell," 14, 22–23; *Dictionary of North Carolina Biography*, s.v. "Caswell, Richard"; Clayton Brown Alexander, *"The First of Patriots and Best of Men": Richard Caswell in Public Life*, edited and annotated by W. Keats Sparrow (Kinston: Lenoir County Colonial Commission, 2007), xvi–xvii, 7, 9. The book is an annotated—with some corrections—version of Alexander's dissertation and is the copy referenced in the present study. Hereinafter it is cited as Alexander and Sparrow, *Richard Caswell in Public Life*.
5. Alexander, "Training of Richard Caswell," 23–24; Alexander and Sparrow, *Richard Caswell in Public Life*, 10, 36; William S. Powell and Michael Hill, eds., *The North Carolina Gazetteer*, 2nd ed. (Chapel Hill: University of North Carolina Press, 2010), 284.
6. Alexander, "Training of Richard Caswell," 24–26; Alexander and Sparrow, *Richard Caswell in Public Life*, 26–28, 35–39; Paul Branch, "Fort Dobbs," in William S. Powell, ed., *Encyclopedia of North Carolina* (Chapel Hill: University of North Carolina Press, 2006), 459.
7. Alexander, "Training of Richard Caswell," 27–28.
8. William L. Saunders, ed., *The Colonial Records of North Carolina*, 10 vols. (Raleigh: State of North Carolina, 1886–90), 10:785; Alexander and Sparrow, *Richard Caswell in Public Life*, 14–15.
9. *Dictionary of North Carolina Biography*, s.v. "Caswell, Richard."
10. Alexander, "Training of Richard Caswell," 28–30; Hugh T. Lefler and William S. Powell, *Colonial North Carolina: A History* (New York: Charles Scribner's Sons, 1973), 256.
11. Alexander, "Training of Richard Caswell," 31.
12. Saunders, *Colonial Records of North Carolina*, 9:31, 779.
13. Lefler and Powell, *Colonial North Carolina*, 256–57.
14. Ron Chernow, *George Washington: A Life* (London: Penguin Books, 2011), 147–48.
15. Robert Middlekauff, *The Glorious Cause: The American Revolution, 1763–1789*, revised ed. (New York: Oxford University Press, 2005), 122–24.
16. Alexander and Sparrow, *Richard Caswell in Public Life*, 8.
17. Thornton W. Mitchell, "Granville Grant and District," and David Southern and Louis P. Towles, "Land Grants," in Powell, *Encyclopedia of North Carolina*, 524, 661–63; *Dictionary of North Carolina Biography*, s.v. "Corbin, Francis"; Ekirch, *"Poor Carolina,"* 133–41.
18. Saunders, *Colonial Records of North Carolina*, 5:19, 1090.
19. Henry Steele Commager, ed., *Documents of American History*, 7th ed. (New York: Appleton-Century-Crofts, 1963), 47–50; Fred Anderson, *Crucible of War: The Seven Years War and the Fate of Empire in British North America, 1754–1766* (New York: Random House, 2001), 594–95, 731.
20. Gordon S. Wood, *The American Revolution: A History* (New York: Modern Library, 2003), 22.

21. *Dictionary of North Carolina Biography*, s.v. "Henderson, Richard"; Wiley J. Williams, "Transylvania Company," in Powell, *Encyclopedia of North Carolina*, 1131; John Preston Arthur, *Western North Carolina: A History from 1730 to 1913* (1914; reprint, Johnson City, TN: Overmountain Press, 1996), 90–92.
22. Saunders, *Colonial Records of North Carolina*, 9:1123–25.
23. Ibid., 10:324.
24. Arthur, *Western North Carolina*, 92; Alexander and Sparrow, *Richard Caswell in Public Life*, 28–29.
25. Alexander and Sparrow, *Richard Caswell in Public Life*, 5; Alan D. Watson, *A History of New Bern and Craven County* (New Bern: Tryon Palace Commission, 1987), 35, 162.
26. *First Census of the United States, 1790: North Carolina* (Washington, D.C.: Government Printing Office, 1908), 137.
27. Will of Richard Caswell, 1790, Dobbs County Original Wills, Records of the North Carolina Secretary of State, State Archives, North Carolina Office of Archives and History, Raleigh.
28. Bill of Sale, April 28, 1781, Richard Caswell Papers, Private Collections, State Archives.
29. Ekirch, *"Poor Carolina,"* 23.

CHAPTER 2

1. Alexander, "Training of Richard Caswell, 17, 21–22; Corbitt, *Formation of the North Carolina Counties*, 89–90.
2. The most recent and analytical full studies of the Regulator movement are Marjoleine Kars, *Breaking Loose Together: The Regulator Rebellion in Pre-Revolutionary North Carolina* (Chapel Hill: University of North Carolina Press, 2002), and Carole Watterson Troxler, *Farming Dissenters: The Regulator Movement in Piedmont North Carolina* (Raleigh: North Carolina Office of Archives and History, 2011).
3. William S. Powell, *North Carolina Through Four Centuries* (Chapel Hill: University of North Carolina Press, 1989), 153–54.
4. Kars, *Breaking Loose Together*, 139–60; Troxler, *Farming Dissenters*, 62–64, 73–75.
5. Kars, *Breaking Loose Together*, 174–75, 183–88.
6. William Tryon to Caswell, November 30, 1770, in William S. Powell, ed., *The Correspondence of William Tryon and Other Selected Papers*, 2 vols. (Raleigh: North Carolina Office of Archives and History, 1980–81), 2:525.
7. Tryon to Caswell, February 19, 1771, in Powell, *Correspondence of William Tryon*, 2:612.
8. Caswell to Tryon, February 20, 1771, in Powell, *Correspondence of William Tryon*, 2:613.

9. Powell, *North Carolina Through Four Centuries*, 156–57; Tryon to "Commanders of the Militia, March 19, 1771" and "Quota of Troops to be Raised, March 19, 1771," in Powell, *Correspondence of William Tryon*, 2:641–44.
10. Tryon to Caswell, April 4, 1771, and "William Tryon's Note Concerning a Letter to Richard Caswell, April 4, 1771," in Powell, *Correspondence of William Tryon*, 2:653.
11. Kars, *Breaking Loose Together*, 197–99. Powell gives Tryon's militia force as "1,452 men, of whom 1,068 came from the east," and the Regulators' strength at 2,000 men. Powell, *North Carolina Through Four Centuries*, 157.
12. "Line of Battle, May 15, 1771," in Powell, *Correspondence of William Tryon*, 2:694.
13. Kars, *Breaking Loose Together*, 199–203.
14. Ibid., 202–07; "Return of the Army Whilst at Herman Husbands on Sandy Creek, May 22, 1771" and "After Orders, June 20, 1771," in Powell, *Correspondence of William Tryon*, 2:714, 747.
15. *Virginia Gazette* (Williamsburg), August 29, 1771.
16. Ibid.

CHAPTER 3

1. Wood, *American Revolution*, 17–18; Hugh F. Rankin, *North Carolina in the American Revolution* (Raleigh: North Carolina Office of Archives and History, 2001), 1–2.
2. Hugh Talmage Lefler and Albert Ray Newsome, *North Carolina: The History of a Southern State* (Chapel Hill: University of North Carolina Press, 1976), 196–97; Edward Smith et al., "Stamp Act," in Powell, *Encyclopedia of North Carolina*, 1069–70.
3. Rankin, *North Carolina in the American Revolution*, 2.
4. Mark M. Boatner III, *Encyclopedia of the American Revolution* (New York: David McKay Co., 1974), 94–95, 810, 1110; Edmund S. Morgan, *The Birth of the Republic, 1763–89*, 3rd ed. (Chicago: University of Chicago Press, 1992), 47, 49.
5. Morgan, *Birth of the Republic*, 50–60.
6. Powell, *North Carolina Through Four Centuries*, 168; Watson, *New Bern and Craven County*, 73.
7. Lefler and Newsome, *North Carolina*, 200.
8. Ibid., 201–02.
9. C.B. Alexander, "Richard Caswell: Versatile Leader of the Revolution," *North Carolina Historical Review* 23 (April 1946): 119; Alexander and Sparrow, *Richard Caswell in Public Life*, 42.
10. Saunders, *Colonial Records of North Carolina*, 10:232.

11. Journal of William Caswell, 1774, Richard Caswell Papers, Private Collections, State Archives. Talmage C. Johnson and Charles R. Holloman have noted that William Caswell's journal frequently has been mistakenly attributed to his father. Johnson and Holloman, *Story of Kinston and Lenoir County*, 42. The "Canady Bill" probably refers to the Quebec Act of June 22, 1774, by which the British government extended the Canadian province of Quebec "into the Mississippi Valley as far south as the Ohio River" and which angered the colonists. Morgan, *Birth of the Republic*, 60, 118. The Bishop of St. Asaph was Jonathan Shipley, who in Parliament opposed sanctions against Boston. *Dictionary of National Biography*, s.v. "Shipley, Jonathan."
12. Silas Deane to Mrs. Deane, September 23, 1774, in Edmund C. Burnett, ed., *Letters of the Members of the Continental Congress*, 8 vols. (Washington, D.C.: Carnegie Institution of Washington, 1921–36), 1:45.
13. David T. Morgan and William J. Schmidt, "From Economic Sanctions to Political Separation: The North Carolina Delegation to the Continental Congress, 1774–1776," *North Carolina Historical Review* 52 (Summer 1975): 216–22; Journal of William Caswell, 1774; Johnson and Holloman, *Story of Kinston and Lenoir County*, 42–44.
14. Wood, *American Revolution*, 49; Carmine Miner Smith, "Committees of Safety," in Powell, *Encyclopedia of North Carolina*, 259–60.
15. Watson, *New Bern and Craven County*, 74.
16. Powell, *North Carolina Through Four Centuries*, 172–74.
17. Wood, *American Revolution*, 53–54; Morgan, *Birth of the Republic*, 68.
18. Powell, *North Carolina Through Four Centuries*, 176–77.
19. Watson, *New Bern and Craven County*, 76–77; Powell, *North Carolina Through Four Centuries*, 176.
20. Morgan and Schmidt, "From Economic Sanctions to Political Separation," 220–21.
21. Richard Caswell to William Caswell, May 11, 1775, Richard Caswell Papers, Private Collections, State Archives.
22. Chernow, *Washington: A Life*, 186, 192–93; Morgan, *Birth of the Republic*, 68–69; Wood, *American Revolution*, 54–55.
23. Alexander, "Richard Caswell: Versatile Leader of the Revolution," 122–23.
24. Richard Cogdell to Caswell, June 18, 1775, Richard Cogdell Papers, Private Collections, State Archives.
25. Morgan and Schmidt, "From Economic Sanctions to Political Separation," 222.
26. Joseph Hewes to Samuel Johnston, July 8, 1775, in Burnett, *Letters of the Members of the Continental Congress*, 1:160.
27. Lindley S. Butler, "Provincial Congresses," in Powell, *Encyclopedia of North Carolina*, 917–18; Powell, *North Carolina Through Four Centuries*, 177, 186.

28. Morgan and Schmidt, "From Economic Sanctions to Political Separation," 224–25.
29. Saunders, *Colonial Records of North Carolina*, 10:148, 232.
30. Wood, *American Revolution*, 55.
31. Walter Clark, ed., *The State Records of North Carolina*, 16 vols. (11–26) (Raleigh: State of North Carolina, 1895–1906), 15:685–87.
32. Rankin, *North Carolina in the American Revolution*, 11–12; Hugh Rankin, *The North Carolina Continentals*, 2nd ed. (Chapel Hill: University of North Carolina Press, 2005), 33–34.
33. Rankin, *North Carolina Continentals*, 33, 35–38, 40.
34. Rankin, *North Carolina in the American Revolution*, 13; Rankin, *North Carolina Continentals*, 39.
35. Rankin, *North Carolina Continentals*, 40–41.
36. Rankin, *North Carolina in the American Revolution*, 14–16; Rankin, *North Carolina Continentals*, 42–45.
37. Rankin, *North Carolina in the American Revolution*, 16.
38. Rankin, *North Carolina Continentals*, 47–52.
39. Ibid., 57–61.
40. Ibid., 53–54.
41. Diary of Richard Smith, March 21, 1776, in Burnett, *Letters of the Members of the Continental Congress*, 1:402.
42. R.D.W. Connor, *Revolutionary Leaders of North Carolina* (Greensboro: North Carolina State Normal and Industrial College, 1916), 93.
43. Powell, *North Carolina Through Four Centuries*, 182–84; Wood, *American Revolution*, 65.
44. Lefler and Newsome, *North Carolina*, 218–20; Robert L. Ganyard, "Radicals and Conservatives in Revolutionary North Carolina: A Point at Issue, the October Election, 1776," *William and Mary Quarterly* 24 (October 1967): 568–69; Alexander, "Richard Caswell: Versatile Leader of the Revolution," 127.
45. Lefler and Newsome, *North Carolina*, 218–20.
46. Ibid., 221–26; Clark, *State Records of North Carolina*, 23:980–84.
47. Ganyard, "Radicals and Conservatives in Revolutionary North Carolina," 570.
48. Milton Ready, *The Tar Heel State: A History of North Carolina* (Columbia: University of South Carolina Press, 2005), 117–18. In another recent history of North Carolina, author William A. Link does not reach a conclusion about which faction dominated the congress but states that the "congress split into conservative and radical factions" and labored under "this conservative-radical power struggle." William A. Link, *North Carolina: Change and Tradition in a Southern State* (Wheeling, IL: Harlan Davidson, 2009), 109.

CHAPTER 4

1. *Virginia Gazette*, January 31, 1777.
2. Ibid.
3. Powell, *North Carolina Through Four Centuries*, 187; Rankin, *North Carolina in the American Revolution*, 27–28; Johnson and Holloman, *Story of Kinston and Lenoir County*, 67.
4. Boatner, *Encyclopedia of the American Revolution*, 98, 197–205; Rankin, *North Carolina in the American Revolution*, 29–30; Rankin, *North Carolina Continentals*, 70–99.
5. Rankin, *North Carolina in the American Revolution*, 30; Boatner, *Encyclopedia of the American Revolution*, 719–25.
6. Alexander, "Richard Caswell: Versatile Leader of the Revolution," 127.
7. Clark, *State Records of North Carolina*, 11:495.
8. Caswell to Thomas Burke, July 15, 1777, Richard Caswell Papers, Southern Historical Collection, Wilson Library, University of North Carolina at Chapel Hill.
9. John Penn, Thomas Burke and William Sharpe to Caswell, July 15, 1779, Richard Caswell Papers, Southern Historical Collection.
10. David T. Morgan, "Cornelius Harnett: Revolutionary Leader and Delegate to the Continental Congress," *North Carolina Historical Review* 49 (July 1972): 236.
11. Rawlins Lowndes to Caswell, November 18, 1778, Richard Caswell Papers, Southern Historical Collection.
12. Alexander, "Richard Caswell: Versatile Leader of the Revolution," 135–36.
13. Clark, *State Records of North Carolina*, 13:42.
14. Caswell to Justices of Craven County, February 6, 1778, Aubrey Lee Brooks Papers, Private Collections, State Archives.
15. Caswell to George Washington, February 15, 1778, in Philander D. Chase et al., eds., *The Papers of George Washington: Revolutionary War Series*, 22 vols. (Charlottesville: University of Virginia Press, 1985–2013), 13:544–45.
16. Washington to Caswell, March 28, 1778, in Chase et al., *Papers of George Washington: Revolutionary War Series*, 14:332.
17. Caswell to Washington, May 6, 1778, in Chase et al., *Papers of George Washington: Revolutionary War Series*, 15:57–58.
18. Rankin, *North Carolina Continentals*, 178.
19. Ibid., 181, 183; Alexander and Sparrow, *Richard Caswell in Public Life*, 73 (quotation).
20. Alexander, "Richard Caswell: Versatile Leader of the Revolution," 133, 137; R.L. Hilldrup, "The Salt Supply of North Carolina During the Revolution," *North Carolina Historical Review* 22 (October 1945): 393–417;

John Penn to Caswell, June 25, 1777, Thomas Addison Emmet Collection, Private Collections, State Archives.

21. Washington to Caswell, March 28, 1778, in Chase et al., *Papers of George Washington: Revolutionary War Series*, 14:332.

22. Alexander, "Richard Caswell: Versatile Leader of the Revolution," 130–31; Theda Perdue and Christopher Arris Oakley, *Native Carolinians: The Indians of North Carolina* (Raleigh: North Carolina Office of Archives and History, 2010), 38–39; William L. Anderson, Ruth Y. Wetmore and John L. Bell, "Cherokee Indians," in Powell, *Encyclopedia of North Carolina*, 209.

23. Clark, *State Records of North Carolina*, 14:678.

24. Caswell to Washington, May 6, 1778, in Chase et al., *Papers of George Washington: Revolutionary War Series*, 15:57–58.

25. Caswell to Henry Laurens, May 6, 1778, Governors Papers, Richard Caswell, State Archives; Boatner, *Encyclopedia of the American Revolution*, 155–58.

26. Caswell to Washington, September 14, 1778, in Chase et al., *Papers of George Washington: Revolutionary War Series*, 16:607–08. See also Clark, *State Records of North Carolina*, 12:873–74.

27. Clark, *State Records of North Carolina*, 11:138, 14:678.

28. Alexander, "Richard Caswell: Versatile Leader of the Revolution," 132–33; Watson, *New Bern and Craven County*, 88–91; Alan D. Watson, *Wilmington, North Carolina, to 1861* (Jefferson, NC: McFarland and Co., 2003), 90–91.

29. John L. Bell, "Confiscation Acts," and Carole Watterson Troxler, "Loyalists," in Powell, *Encyclopedia of North Carolina*, 274, 697–99; Rankin, *North Carolina in the American Revolution*, 34–35, 41–44; Alexander, "Richard Caswell: Versatile Leader of the Revolution," 133–34; Alexander and Sparrow, *Richard Caswell in Public Life*, 82–83.

30. Alexander, "Richard Caswell: Versatile Leader of the Revolution," 139–41; Boatner, *Encyclopedia of the American Revolution*, 262–63, 705–07.

31. Caswell to Washington, February 15, 1778, in Chase et al., *Papers of George Washington: Revolutionary War Series*, 13:544–45.

32. Caswell to Washington, November 25, 1777, in Chase et al., *Papers of George Washington: Revolutionary War Series*, 12:385–86.

33. Washington to Caswell, December 25, 1777, in Chase et al., *Papers of George Washington: Revolutionary War Series*, 12:703.

34. Alexander, "Richard Caswell: Versatile Leader of the Revolution," 139–41; Boatner, *Encyclopedia of the American Revolution*, 262–63, 705–07.

35. Rankin, *North Carolina Continentals*, 184–89; Boatner, *Encyclopedia of the American Revolution*, 46, 522, 636.

36. John Richard Alden, *The South in the Revolution, 1763–1789* (Baton Rouge: Louisiana State University Press, 1957), 232–35.

37. Rankin, *North Carolina Continentals*, 191–92.

38. Boatner, *Encyclopedia of the American Revolution*, 113–14, 980–88, 1034–36, 1062.

39. Rankin, *North Carolina Continentals*, 200, 209; Johnson and Holloman, *Story of Kinston and Lenoir County*, 68–69. Apparently, the John Barefoot mentioned in Rankin was one of the local persons who heard about Bass's statement.
40. Boatner, *Encyclopedia of the American Revolution*, 205, 208; Rankin, *North Carolina in the American Revolution*, 31–32.
41. Boatner, *Encyclopedia of the American Revolution*, 287–89.
42. Michael Hill, ed., *The Governors of North Carolina* (Raleigh: North Carolina Office of Archives and History, 2007), 25–26, 111–12; *Dictionary of North Carolina Biography*, s.v. "Caswell, Richard"; Alexander and Sparrow, *Richard Caswell in Public Life*, 11.

Chapter 5

1. Clark, *State Records of North Carolina*, 14:811; Rankin, *North Carolina Continentals*, 235.
2. Boatner, *Encyclopedia of the American Revolution*, 159, 165.
3. C.B. Alexander, "Richard Caswell's Military and Later Public Services," *North Carolina Historical Review* 23 (July 1946): 289–90.
4. Horatio Gates to Caswell, August 4, 1780, Richard Caswell Papers, Private Collections, State Archives.
5. Rankin, *North Carolina Continentals*, 242.
6. Boatner, *Encyclopedia of the American Revolution*, 412.
7. Alexander, "Richard Caswell's Military and Later Public Services," 290–91; Rankin, *North Carolina Continentals*, 242.
8. Rankin, *North Carolina Continentals*, 244; Boatner, *Encyclopedia of the American Revolution*, 165–69.
9. Otho Holland Williams, "A Narrative of the Campaign of 1780," excerpted in Ed Southern, ed., *Voices of the American Revolution in the Carolinas* (Winston-Salem, NC: John F. Blair Publisher, 2009), 112.
10. Caswell to Abner Nash, August 19, 1780, Richard Caswell Papers, Private Collections, State Archives.
11. Ibid.
12. Alexander, "Richard Caswell's Military and Later Public Services," 294–95.
13. Rankin, *North Carolina in the American Revolution*, 39–45.
14. Alexander, "Richard Caswell's Military and Later Public Services," 294–96; Boatner, *Encyclopedia of the American Revolution*, 1076–77.
15. Rankin, *North Carolina Continentals*, 246.
16. George W. Troxler, "Board of War," in Powell, *Encyclopedia of North Carolina*, 136–37; Rankin, *North Carolina Continentals*, 246–47.

17. Rankin, *North Carolina Continentals*, 255.
18. Alexander, "Richard Caswell's Military and Later Public Services," 296–97; Alexander and Sparrow, *Richard Caswell in Public Life*, 112–13.
19. Alden, *South in the Revolution*, 251–54; Rankin, *North Carolina in the American Revolution*, 45–48.
20. Jeffrey J. Crow, *A Chronicle of North Carolina during the American Revolution, 1763–1789* (Raleigh: North Carolina Office of Archives and History, 1997), 44–45; Alexander, "Richard Caswell's Military and Later Public Services," 297–98; Rankin, *North Carolina Continentals*, 268–318; Alexander and Sparrow, *Richard Caswell in Public Life*, 113.
21. Crow, *Chronicle of North Carolina during the American Revolution*, 46–47; Middlekauff, *Glorious Cause*, 497–501; Boatner, *Encyclopedia of the American Revolution*, 353–56.
22. Watson, *Wilmington, North Carolina, to 1861*, 91; Rankin, *North Carolina in the American Revolution*, 61; *Dictionary of North Carolina Biography*, s.vv. "Ashe, John" and "Harnett, Cornelius."
23. Boatner, *Encyclopedia of the American Revolution*, 288, 865; Crow, *Chronicle of North Carolina during the American Revolution*, 47–48; Middlekauff, *Glorious Cause*, 579–80.
24. Rankin, *North Carolina in the American Revolution*, 62–63.
25. Alexander, "Richard Caswell's Military and Later Public Services," 298; Watson, *Wilmington, North Carolina, to 1861*, 93.
26. Alexander and Sparrow, *Richard Caswell in Public Life*, 115–16; *Dictionary of North Carolina Biography*, s.vv. "Ashe, John" and "Ashe, Samuel"; Abner Nash to William Caswell, May 28, 1780, William Caswell Papers, Private Collections, State Archives.
27. Clark, *State Records of North Carolina*, 22:1023–35.
28. Nash to William Caswell, May 28, 1780, William Caswell Papers.
29. William Caswell to Loyalists, May 31, 1781, Draper Manuscripts, Private Collections, State Archives.
30. Carole Watterson Troxler, *The Loyalist Experience in North Carolina* (Raleigh: North Carolina Office of Archives and History, 1976); *Dictionary of North Carolina Biography*, s.v. "Fanning, David"; Hill, *Governors of North Carolina*, 15–16; Crow, *Chronicle of North Carolina during the American Revolution*, 51.
31. Middlekauff, *Glorious Cause*, 580–90.
32. Watson, *Wilmington, North Carolina, to 1861*, 93.
33. Middlekauff, *Glorious Cause*, 590–602.
34. Boatner, *Encyclopedia of the American Revolution*, 849.

CHAPTER 6

1. Alexander, "Richard Caswell's Military and Later Public Services," 298–301; Alexander and Sparrow, *Richard Caswell in Public Life*, 116–17; Alden, *South in the Revolution*, 351; Kevin T. Barksdale, *The Lost State of Franklin: America's First Secession* (Lexington: University Press of Kentucky, 2009), 64–65, 83–90.
2. Caswell to William Caswell, May 3, 1784, Richard Caswell Papers, Southern Historical Collection.
3. Caswell to B[rigadier] G[eneral William] Caswell, April 27, 1784, Richard Caswell Papers, Southern Historical Collection.
4. Charles D. Rodenbough, *Governor Alexander Martin: Biography of a North Carolina Revolutionary Statesman* (Jefferson, NC: McFarland and Co., 2004), 81–82. Rodenbough sometimes gives Maclaine's first name as Alexander, and it appears as such in his book's index. On Maclaine, see *Dictionary of North Carolina Biography*, s.v. "Maclaine, Archibald," and Watson, *Wilmington, North Carolina, to 1861*, 19, 49, 80, 81, 94–95, 96.
5. Rodenbough, *Governor Alexander Martin*, 98.
6. Alexander and Sparrow, *Richard Caswell in Public Life*, 124.
7. Alexander, "Richard Caswell's Military and Later Public Services," 301–03; Clark, *State Records of North Carolina*, 22:124, 642–47; Lefler and Newsome, *North Carolina*, 274–76.
8. Clark, *State Records of North Carolina*, 17:446–49.
9. Ibid., 17:427; Barksdale, *Lost State of Franklin*, 61, 65.
10. Alexander, "Richard Caswell's Military and Later Public Services," 302–03.
11. Clark, *State Records of North Carolina*, 17:427–28.
12. Ibid., 22:649–50.
13. George W. Troxler, "Franklin, State of," in Powell, *Encyclopedia of North Carolina*, 468–70; "Treaty with the Cherokee, 1785," in Charles J. Kappler, ed., *Indian Affairs: Laws and Treaties*, 2 vols. (Washington, D.C.: Government Printing Office, 1904), 2:8–11.
14. Barksdale, *Lost State of Franklin*, 84–90 (quotations on 85 and 86).
15. Ibid., 90; Alexander and Sparrow, *Richard Caswell in Public Life*, 132–33; Thomas Evans to Caswell, November 10, 25, 1787, Governors Papers, Richard Caswell, State Archives.
16. Joseph J. Ellis, *American Creation: Triumphs and Tragedies at the Founding of the Republic* (New York: Random House, 2007), 140–64.
17. Barksdale, *Lost State of Franklin*, 108–117 (quotation on 110).
18. "Treaty with the Cherokee, 1791," in Kappler, *Indian Affairs: Laws and Treaties*, 2:29–33; Robert W. Remini, *Andrew Jackson and the Course of American Freedom* (New York: Harper and Row, 1981), 220–22, 257–79.

19. Kristofer Ray, "Leadership, Loyalty, and Sovereignty in the Revolutionary American Southwest: The State of Franklin as a Test Case," *North Carolina Historical Review* 92 (April 2015): 139–44.
20. Clark, *State Records of North Carolina*, 20:707.
21. Lefler and Newsome, *North Carolina*, 276; Powell, *North Carolina Through Four Centuries*, 219–21; *Dictionary of North Carolina Biography*, s.v. "Sevier, John."
22. Boatner, *Encyclopedia of the American Revolution*, 35; Middlekauff, *Glorious Cause*, 640–41.
23. Middlekauff, *Glorious Cause*, 641.
24. Boatner, *Encyclopedia of the American Revolution*, 849; George C. Herring, *From Colony to Superpower: U.S. Foreign Relations since 1776* (New York: Oxford University Press, 2008), 41; Middlekauff, *Glorious Cause*, 590–95, 607; Gordon S. Wood, *Empire of Liberty: A History of the Early Republic* (New York: Oxford University Press, 2009), 15.
25. Clark, *State Records of North Carolina*, 17:427.
26. Herring, *From Colony to Superpower*, 35.
27. Wood, *Empire of Liberty*, 15.
28. Alexander, "Richard Caswell's Military and Later Public Services," 307.
29. Clark, *State Records of North Carolina*, 20:668–73.
30. Ibid., 20:716.
31. Herring, *From Colony to Superpower*, 35.
32. Alexander, "Richard Caswell's Military and Later Public Services," 307–08; Joseph J. Ellis, *The Quartet: Orchestrating the Second American Revolution* (New York: Alfred A. Knopf, 2015), 80–81 (quotation on 81).
33. Caswell to James Bowdoin, June 21, 1786, Richard Caswell Papers, Private Collections, State Archives.
34. Lefler and Newsome, *North Carolina*, 277–78; Middlekauff, *Glorious Cause*, 620–21.
35. Middlekauff, *Glorious Cause*, 620–21.
36. Ibid., 641; Ellis, *Quartet*, 81.
37. Lefler and Newsome, *North Carolina*, 279.
38. A.R. Newsome, "North Carolina and the Ratification of the Federal Constitution," *North Carolina Historical Review* 17 (October 1940): 288.
39. William S. Powell, "Constitution, U.S., Signers of," in Powell, *Encyclopedia of North Carolina*, 286.
40. Lefler and Newsome, *North Carolina*, 279.
41. Middlekauff, *Glorious Cause*, 642–44.
42. Wood, *Empire of Liberty*, 19.
43. Thomas Jefferson, "Answers and Observations for Démeunier's Article on the United States in . . . 1786," in Jefferson, *Writings*, with notes by Merrill D. Peterson (New York: American Library, 1984), 578.

44. Middlekauff, *Glorious Cause*, 642–46. For Washington's role at the convention, see Edward J. Larson, *The Return of George Washington, 1783–1789* (New York: HarperCollins, 2014), 101–98.
45. Lefler and Newsome, *North Carolina*, 279–81.
46. Alexander and Sparrow, *Richard Caswell in Public Life*, 137.
47. Clark, *State Records of North Carolina*, 20:723, 752–54, 763.
48. Ibid., 20:752.
49. Ibid., 20:723–24.
50. Middlekauff, *Glorious Cause*, 668; Powell, *North Carolina Through Four Centuries*, 224; Larson, *Return of George Washington*, 173, 176, 226–27.
51. Clark, *State Records of North Carolina*, 20:763–64.
52. Ibid., 20:764, 766.
53. Morgan, *Birth of the Republic*, 143.
54. Price, *"There Ought to Be a Bill of Rights,"* 13–14.
55. Newsome, "North Carolina and the Ratification of the Federal Constitution," 291–92.
56. Stephen E. Massengill, *North Carolina Votes on the Constitution: A Roster of Delegates to the State Ratification Conventions of 1788 and 1789* (Raleigh: North Carolina Office of Archives and History, 1988), xi, 10; John L. Cheney Jr., *North Carolina Government, 1585–1979: A Narrative and Statistical History* (Raleigh: North Carolina Department of Secretary of State, 1981), 220; Ellis, *Quartet*, 173; Charles Johnston to James Iredell, November 14, 1788, in Don Higginbotham, Donna Kelly and Lang Baradell, eds., *The Papers of James Iredell*, 3 vols. (Raleigh: North Carolina Office of Archives and History, 1976–2003), 3:449–50.
57. Price, *"There Ought to Be a Bill of Rights,"* 1–2.
58. Ibid., 14–15; John C. Cavanagh, *Decision at Fayetteville: The North Carolina Ratification Convention and General Assembly of 1789* (Raleigh: North Carolina Office of Archives and History, 1989), 26–29; Morgan, *Birth of the Republic*, 155, 195.
59. Cavanagh, *Decision at Fayetteville*, 21–22.
60. *State Gazette of North Carolina* (Edenton), December 3, 1789.
61. Ibid., December 4, 1788.
62. Ibid., December 3, 1789.
63. Cavanagh, *Decision at Fayetteville*, 22; *Dictionary of North Carolina Biography*, s.v. "Caswell, Richard."
64. William Blount to William White, November 22, 1789, in Alice Barnwell Keith, William Masterson and David T. Morgan, eds., *The John Gray Blount Papers, 1764–1833*, 4 vols. (Raleigh: North Carolina Office of Archives and History, 1952–82), 1:517–18.
65. *State Gazette of North Carolina*, December 17, 1789.
66. *Dictionary of North Carolina Biography*, s.v. "Caswell, Richard."

67. Will of Richard Caswell, 1790; Alexander and Sparrow, *Richard Caswell in Public Life*, xxii, 141, 185.

Epilogue

1. Wood, *American Revolution*, 67.
2. Alexander and Sparrow, *Richard Caswell in Public Life*, 61.

Index

D

M

N

O

P

Q

R

S

T

About the Author

Joe Mobley teaches North Carolina history at North Carolina State University in Raleigh. He is the author of a number of books related to the history of the state. In 2006, he received the North Caroliniana Book Award, which is presented annually for the best book on the history of North Carolina. His other titles for The History Press are *Raleigh, North Carolina: A Brief History* (2009) and *Confederate Generals of North Carolina: Tar Heels in Command* (2011). Mobley has served as president of the North Carolina Literary and Historical Association and of the Historical Society of North Carolina.